An Ounce of Prevention Plus a Pound of Cure!
Tests and Techniques for Aiding Individual Readers

GOODYEAR EDUCATION SERIES
Theodore W. Hipple, Editor; University of South Carolina at Spartanburg

CHANGE FOR CHILDREN
Sandra N. Kaplan, Jo Ann B. Kaplan, Sheila K. Madsen,
Bette K. Taylor

CREATING A LEARNING ENVIRONMENT
Ethel Breyfogle, Pamela Santich, Ronald Kremer,
Susan Nelson, Carol Pitts

DO YOU READ ME?
Arnold Griese

IMAGINE THAT!
Joyce King and Carol Katzman

THE LANGUAGE ARTS IDEA BOOK
Joanne D. Schaff

THE LEARNING CENTER BOOK
Tom Davidson, Phyllis Fountain, Rachel Grogan, Verl Short,
Judy Steely, Katherine Freeman

LOVING AND BEYOND
Joe Abruscato and Jack Hassard

MAINSTREAMING LANGUAGE ARTS AND SOCIAL STUDIES
Charles R. Coble, Anne Adams, Paul B. Hounshell

MAINSTREAMING SCIENCE AND MATH
Charles R. Coble, Anne Adams, Paul B. Hounshell

NEW SCHOOLS FOR A NEW AGE
William Georgiades, Reuben Hilde, Grant Macaulay

ONE AT A TIME ALL AT ONCE
Jack E. Blackburn and Conrad Powell

THE OTHER SIDE OF THE REPORT CARD
Larry Chase

AN OUNCE OF PREVENTION PLUS A POUND OF CURE
Ronald W. Bruton

REACHING TEENAGERS
Don Beach

THE READING CORNER
Harry W. Forgan

A SURVIVAL KIT FOR TEACHERS AND PARENTS
Myrtle T. Collins and DWane R. Collins

THE WHOLE COSMOS CATALOG OF SCIENCE ACTIVITIES
Joe Abruscato and Jack Hassard

WILL THE REAL TEACHER PLEASE STAND UP? 2nd edition
Mary C. Greer and Bonnie Rubinstein

A YOUNG CHILD EXPERIENCES
Sandra N. Kaplan, Jo Ann B. Kaplan, Sheila K. Madsen,
Bette K. Gould

An Ounce of Prevention Plus a Pound of Cure:
Tests and Techniques for Aiding Individual Readers

Ronald W. Bruton, Ed.D.

Principal, Central Point School District
Central Point, Oregon

Formerly Assistant Professor of Elementary Education
Indiana State University
Terre Haute, Indiana

Goodyear Publishing Company, Inc.
Santa Monica, California

Library of Congress Cataloging in Publication Data

Bruton, Ronald W.
    An ounce of prevention plus a pound of cure.

    (Goodyear education series)
    1. Reading—Handbooks, manuals, etc. I. Title.
LB1050.B78   428'.4'071   76-20600
ISBN 0-87620-630-5 (paper)
        0-87620-631-3 (case)

Y-6305-0 (paper)
    6313-4 (case)

Current Printing (last digit):
10 9 8 7 6 5 4 3 2

Printed in the United States of America

Production Editor: Janice Gallagher
Copy Editor: Victoria Pasternack
Text and Cover Design: Christy Butterfield
Text Illustrations: Barbara Hack and Bonnie Laurie Russell
Chapter Opener Illustrations: Patrick Maloney

CONTENTS

CHAPTER 5 DECODING: MULTISYLLABIC WORDS 51

will enable you to

1. Diagnose children's general and specific needs for instructions in decoding multisyllabic words
2. Teach children to decode multisyllabic words by using appropriate teaching procedures

CHAPTER 6 MOTIVATION 59

will enable you to

1. Organize the classroom reading program into three essential components
2. Use reinforcement techniques to maximize attainment of skills
3. Minimize unnecessary paper-and-pencil assignments
4. Provide for students' personal interests, individual reading levels, and individual attention spans

CHAPTER 7 BASIC COMPREHENSION: THE DIRECTED READING LESSON 69

will enable you to

1. Improve the child's ability to concentrate on what he is reading
2. Improve the child's ability to read for facts, organizations, and main ideas
3. Increase the child's reading vocabulary
4. Enable the child to understand the meaning of literary devices

CHAPTER 8 VOCABULARY 77

will enable you to

1. Diagnose students' needs for vocabulary instruction
2. Teach vocabulary using one of three methods—the context, word-elements, or language-interaction pattern

ACKNOWLEDGMENTS

I would like to thank several friends and colleagues for their help in writing this book. Special thanks to Professor Carl J. Wallen (my graduate advisor) for teaching me many of the basic concepts of testing and teaching described in this book. Also, special thanks to Mrs. Jane Angell, education editor at Indiana State University, for many editorial suggestions and for constant encouragement. Many thanks to Professors Vanita Gibbs, David Waterman, William G. McCarthy, Donald Hagness, and William Van Till (all at Indiana State University) for their suggestions and other help.

INTRODUCTION

In writing this introduction, I am trying to answer the questions that I asked myself as I wrote the rest of the book—What do teachers really want to know? Here are the questions I thought you'd ask, and my answers.

WHAT'S IN THIS BOOK?

This book has ten parts. Each part begins with the story of a common reading-teaching problem. Next, it presents a brief analysis of the problem and a solution. Most of the solutions involve diagnostic testing, record keeping, and active teaching. Each part ends with a suggested application procedure for readers who identify with the problem, agree with the suggestions, and want to use them to help children.

WHOM IS IT FOR?

Mainly, it's for classroom teachers who want to improve their skills. The book is meant especially for teachers who are trying to individualize reading in an open-concept, nongraded, or continuous-progress school. It explains what I had to learn to individualize instruction in my elementary classroom.

After that, it's for teachers in training. I wrote it for use in a field- and competency-based course in corrective reading. My university students read and applied each of the techniques with children during class time. The book taught them specifically what to do to help children learn to read. They said they liked it. (But then, what do undergraduates tell professors who write?)

HOW IS IT USED?

If you are an elementary teacher working to improve your classroom reading program, you may follow this procedure. Skim through the anecdotes at the beginning of each chapter. Decide which problem is most like yours and read that chapter. After reading, rehearse and perform the application exercise. If applying the technique described helps you work with children more effectively and makes you feel better about yourself as a teacher, then the process is working. Pick another chapter and repeat the process.

The book may be used as an inservice program. One teacher would prepare to lead an inservice meeting by selecting a topic, reading the chapter, rehearsing the technique (perhaps with a friend), and trying it out with children. At the teachers' meeting, the leader might begin by asking participants to analyze the problem in the anecdote: Is it like any of the problems in your classroom? What is being done about it now? Next, he or she might describe personal experiences with the technique and demonstrate it. After that, the leader asks everyone to practice the teaching technique using a different reading skill. Finally, teachers apply the skills in their regular classroom.

In university classes, the techniques are similar. As an instructor, I sometimes ask my students to analyze the problem in the anecdote and tell me what they would do about it. Then, we role-play the techniques. Finally, students apply the techniques with children in a nearby school.

WHAT ARE ITS BIASES?

The book is based on the notion that there are certain basic competencies required to teach in an individualized program. An elementary teacher *must* be able to

1. Identify each child's optimum reading level accurately in order to place him in appropriate material

2. Diagnose basic visual problems (such as nearsightedness, farsightedness, and "lazy-eye") and visual discrimination problems and make referrals or teach as needed

3. Diagnose basic hearing problems and auditory discrimination problems and make referrals or teach as needed

4. Diagnose children's problems with phonic and multisyllabic word attack and do active teaching as needed

5. Diagnose children's knowledge of word meaning and teach word meanings necessary for comprehension

6. Diagnose basic comprehension problems and teach as needed

7. Identify children who have mastered basic comprehension skills and work with them on higher-level comprehension skills, mainly through discussion

8. Motivate children who are turned off to reading through systematic reinforcement, attention to personal interests, and judicious use of seatwork

9. Conduct a series of personal reading conferences that result in diagnostic information, increased motivation, and an improved self-image for the child

These abilities constitute an essential set of competencies for teaching reading. And that is what this book is all about.

It might be useful to note what is left out. The book does not debate issues in reading, document the history of certain practices, describe research studies, or present many opinions of authorities. All these are important, but not as important as acquiring basic teaching competencies.

TEACHING AT AN OPTIMUM LEVEL

will enable you to

1. Administer and score an informal reading inventory

2. Interpret the results for use in grouping, analyzing materials, diagnosing skills and communicating with parents

Beth Anderton was shaken by a parent's angry phone call. "Alan hasn't learned a thing since he's been in your class!" the mother had shouted. "He cries every morning because his schoolbooks are too hard for him to read. How can you tell me that you're helping him when all you do is expect the impossible? My husband and I agreed to retain him in the third grade so that he could work at his own level. But you seem to be making Alan just as miserable as his teacher did last year, and we're sick of it! Either you'll do something about it or my husband and I will go to the school board."

Beth thought back several months. At the beginning of the school year, she had called each child up to her desk to determine which reading group he or she should be placed in. She had asked the child to read from each of three basal readers—at levels 2-2, 3-1, and 3-2—the same readers used for each of three reading groups. She had placed Alan in the low reading group. Alan was neither the best nor the worst in the group. Beth had thought that he was doing all right—until this morning's phone call.

How would you analyze this problem? _____

_____

_____

What would you do about it? _____

_____

_____

You may have identified a number of problems, but one stands out. Alan has not been assigned to the proper level of basal reader. From the brief description of the teacher's method for placing children in appropriate reading groups, it is highly probable that many other children in Mrs. Anderton's classroom are not in appropriate groups either. Consider the fact that she tested the children very casually on only three levels—2-2, 3-1, 3-2. When children at the third-grade level are tested carefully, third graders are found to read at eight or nine different grade equivalent levels—P, 1-1, 1-2, 2-1, 2-2, 3-1, 3-2, 4, and 5. Mrs. Anderton's casual testing procedure has almost certainly resulted in Alan's being placed in an overly difficult level.

Placing children at the optimum level of reading difficulty is essential for successful instruction. Each child should be placed at a level where he can read most of the words and understand the content but still encounter a few unfamiliar words and concepts. Such placement offers him a reasonable challenge conducive to growth in reading skill.

There are two possibilities for error in determining a child's reading level: assigning materials that are either too simple or too difficult. If children are assigned materials that are too easy, they have no opportunity to acquire new reading skills. This is a common occurrence for able and gifted children, who may go unchallenged by classroom instruction for years. In contrast, if children are assigned materials that are too difficult, their frustration becomes so intense that they learn to hate and fear reading. This latter case is probably what has happened to Alan.

ADMINISTERING THE INFORMAL READING INVENTORY

Using an informal reading inventory (referred to as an *IRI*) is an accurate method of placing children at the optimum level for reading instruction. An IRI is an individually administered test of reading performance. An IRI consists of two booklets, one for the student and another for the teacher. The student's copy contains a series of short, graded reading selections corresponding to the levels in a basal reader. A page from the student's copy of an IRI is reproduced in Figure 1-1.

The teacher's copy of an IRI has four parts. First, there is a motivational statement to be read to the student before presenting each selection. Second, the selection from the student's copy is reproduced in the teacher's copy. Third is a list of comprehension questions for the teacher to ask the student. And fourth is a scoring system for evaluating the student's performance. A page from the teacher's copy of an IRI is shown in Figure 1-2.

To administer an IRI, first read the motivational statement aloud to the child. Then ask the child to read the appropriate selection aloud. As the child reads, mark each of his errors with an appropriate symbol (described in the next section). When the child has

---

figure 1-1

A PAGE FROM AN IRI: STUDENT'S COPY

AN AIRPLANE TRIP

Janet and Jim looked out the airplane window. Far below them the trees and houses looked so small that they seemed to be toys.

A little while later, Janet said, "Everything's getting gray now. I can't see the ground any more."

Suddenly there was a flash of light and a very loud noise.

"What was that?" cried Jim.

"Thunder," answered Father.

"We're in a storm now."

The plane started to bounce up and down.

"Oh, Father," said Janet, "we're falling down." And she began to cry.

"We're not falling. We're going higher," said Father.

Soon the plane stopped bouncing. The sun became bright again and the children could see blue sky outside the window. Jim said, "Look at all those dark clouds down there. We got out of the storm by going over it."

From the Pupil Placement Tests *by Sheila K. Hollander and Marian Reisman (New York: Houghton Mifflin, 1970). Reprinted by permission of the publisher.*

---

figure 1-2

A PAGE FROM AN IRI: TEACHER'S COPY

MOTIVATION: Now you will read about a family that took a trip on a plane. Find out what exciting thing happened on the trip.

AN AIRPLANE TRIP

Janet and Jim looked out the airplane window. Far below them the trees and houses looked so small that they seemed to be toys.

A little while later, Janet said, "Everything's getting gray now. I can't see the ground any more."

Suddenly there was a flash of light and a very loud noise.

"What was that?" cried Jim.

"Thunder," answered Father. "We're in a storm now."

The plane started to bounce up and down.

"Oh, Father," said Janet, "we're falling down." And she began to cry.

"We're not falling. We're going higher," said Father.

Soon the plane stopped bouncing. The sun became bright again and the children could see blue sky outside the window. Jim said, "Look at all those dark clouds down there. We got out of the storm by going over it."

COMPREHENSION QUESTIONS

(M) 1. What was the exciting thing that happened on the trip? (The plane got into a thunderstorm.)

(F) 2. How did the plane get out of the thunderstorm? (By going higher and flying over it.)

(S) 3. What did Janet notice just before the loud noise and the flash of light? (That she couldn't see the ground any longer, or that everything had become gray outside.)

(F) 4. What did the houses and trees look like from the plane? (Toys.)

(F) 5. Who was traveling with Janet and Jim? (Father.)

(I) 6. Why did Janet think the plane was falling? (It started bouncing up and down.)

(I) 7. How did Janet feel when the plane was bouncing up and down? (Afraid, frightened, scared.)

(I) 8. How did Father know they were in a thunderstorm? (By the flash of light and the loud noise.)

(V) 9. What does *ground* mean in this story? (The earth where we live.)

(F) 10. How did Jim know they had flown above the storm? (He could see a lot of dark clouds beneath the plane.)

Note: The *Pupil Placement Tests* also include an error-scoring system on the marking copy.

From the Pupil Placement Tests *by Sheila K. Hollander and Marian Reisman (New York: Houghton Mifflin, 1970). Reprinted by permission of the publisher.*

---

finished reading aloud, ask him each of the comprehension questions and record his responses. When the child has finished these tasks, evaluate his proficiency to determine whether he should read the next selection. Repeat the procedure at each subsequent reading level. Stop testing when it becomes apparent that the child is having great difficulty with a selection.

A Scoring System

Developing a specific and consistent system for marking children's errors on the teacher's copy of an IRI is important for several reasons. It will help you determine quickly a child's areas of difficulty and permit you to plan instruction accordingly. It will enable you to communicate the problem more clearly to the child's parents and to other teachers. And finally, a clear and consistent marking system will enable you to assess the child's progress during the time you have been instructing him.

The following are the kinds of errors children often make and a corresponding set of appropriate marks for use on the teacher's copy of the IRI.

Omissions. Sometimes children omit parts of words, whole words, phrases, or punctuation. In this event, circle the omitted item. For example:

The material:	"John went into the store."
Child's response:	"John went the store."
Appropriate mark:	"John went (into) the store."

Pronunciations. Sometimes children will not attempt to read a word they are unsure of and will, by their behavior, indicate they want you to help them. For example:

The material:	"The lad walked up the gangway."
Child's response:	"The lad walked up the" (looks to you for help).
Teacher:	"Gangway."
Appropriate mark:	"The lad walked up the ^(P) gangway."

Substitutions. Sometimes children substitute a different word for the one in the text. For example:

The material:	"It was an octagon."
Child's response:	"It was an octopus."
Appropriate mark:	"It was an ~~octagon~~." (octopus written above)

Substitutions may or may not interfere with reading comprehension. The substitution of the word *octopus* for *octagon* certainly does interfere, and the error should be recorded. But children sometimes substitute equivalent function words, such as *a* for *the*, that do not change the meaning of the text or interfere with comprehension in the least. For example:

The material:	"The boy was going home."
Child's response:	"A boy was going home."

Since the change is minor, it is probably best to ignore it.

Repetitions. Occasionally children repeat a word or a phrase. If the repetition is substantial, perhaps a phrase or more, it should be recorded. For example:

The material:	"They were going through the tunnel on the south side of Mount Shasta."
Child's response:	"They were going through the tunnel . . . were going through the tunnel on the south side of Mount Shasta."
Appropriate mark:	"They were going through the tunnel on the south side of Mount Shasta."

Here again, the child's reading behavior may or may not interfere with comprehension. If you believe that the repetition is minor and does not interfere with comprehension, you may ignore it. If repetitions are lengthy or frequent, however, be sure to mark them since they probably will interfere with comprehension.

Hesitations. Sometimes children hesitate often enough and long enough that it will interfere with comprehension. If you believe this to be the case, mark each hesitation error. For example:

The material:	"The burglars seemed to know just where the jewels were."
Child's response:	"The . . . bur . . . glars seemed to know just where the . . . jewels were."
Appropriate mark:	"The burglars seemed to know just where the jewels were."

Since children often read IRI material very rapidly, you should probably know the marking system perfectly before attempting to administer an inventory. You may wish to double-check to ensure that you have memorized the marking system before proceeding.

After the child has finished reading the selection, ask each comprehension question aloud. As he answers, attend very closely to determine whether he understands the selection. Evaluate his responses and mark the teacher's scoring copy accordingly. If the answer is clearly right, simply mark the scoring copy question with a check (✓). If the answer is clearly wrong, mark the scoring copy with a zero (0). But if the child's answer is confusing, you may wish to write it out on the scoring copy for later evaluation.

One reason that a child's answer may be confusing is that children often answer from personal experience rather than from comprehension of the reading selection. For example, if the story is about a plane that flies through a storm, and the question that follows is, "How did the pilot know they were out of the storm?"—the child may answer from his own experience: "The sky looked better." If you believe that the child is answering from experience rather than from having understood the reading selection, it is probably best to score the answer as incorrect. Although this may seem rigid and punitive, it is not actually. It is instead a way of ensuring that the child is not placed at his frustration level in assigned readings on the basis of an overly optimistic test scoring and interpretation.

Determining Functional Reading Levels

After the child has read all of the IRI selections it seems reasonable to ask him to read, and after you have recorded his errors, you will then need to determine his functional reading levels. Begin by computing the percentage of words he read correctly aloud. Here are the computational steps.

1. Count the number of words in each selection and the number of errors the child made.

2. Divide the number of errors by the number of words. (See the following example.)

Number of words in the third reading selection: 127

Number of errors the child made in oral reading: 11

Number of errors divided by the number of words:

$$127 \overline{)11.00}^{.086}$$

3. Round off the decimal to two digits and subtract that amount from 1.00. Then convert the result to a percentage.

$$\begin{array}{r} 1.00 \\ -\ .09 \\ \hline .91 \end{array} = 91\%$$

This percentage (91% in the example) represents the child's word recognition ability.

Next, compute the percentage of comprehension questions the child answered correctly. Here are the computational steps.

1. Count the number of comprehension questions asked and the number of correct answers.

2. Divide the number of correct answers by the number of questions asked.

3. Compute the decimal obtained to a percentage and round off. (See the following example.)

$$\text{(questions asked)} \quad 9\ \overline{)\ 6.\ \text{(correct answers)}}^{\ .6666\ \text{(decimal obtained)}} = 67\%$$

This percentage represents the child's ability to comprehend reading material in the selection he or she has just read. At this point, you have scores for word recognition (91%) and comprehension (67%).

INTERPRETING CHILDREN'S IRI SCORES

Word Recognition

The scores obtained for word recognition and comprehension must be interpreted before the teacher can make instructional decisions. Percentage scores for word recognition may be assigned functional reading levels as follows:

Percentage for Word Recognition	Functional Reading Level
98% to 100%	Independent Reading Level
90% to 97%	Instructional Reading Level
89% or less	Frustration Reading Level

In other words, if the child has a word recognition score of 91% on the reading selection written at the second-grade level, then second grade would be considered his instructional reading level. Each word recognition score has a corresponding functional reading level.

The three functional reading levels—independent, instructional, and frustration—may be interpreted as follows:

Independent Level. At this level, children can read fluently and easily with little or no help. Children should be assigned to materials at this level for most normal assignments when help from the teacher is unavailable. They will probably also enjoy reading library books at this level more than they would books at a harder level. Children should have ready access to many books at their independent reading level.

Instructional Level. At this level, children can read with *some help from the teacher*. Children should be assigned materials at this level only when the teacher is available to teach them new words before they read and to help with difficult words while they are reading. This level has instructional advantages. That is, the child must unlock new words and phrases of moderate difficulty. This challenge produces growth in reading skill.

Frustration Level. At this level, the problems and frustrations of reading are usually too numerous to permit the child to function well. Children often show signs of anxiety and tension when asked to read at their frustration level. It is important for the teacher to know what each child's frustration level is so that he or she can avoid assigning reading at that level, not only during reading instruction but also during social studies, science, or mathematics.

Comprehension

Children's scores on reading comprehension are interpreted similarly to those for word recognition. The functional reading levels for comprehension are as follows:

Percentage for Comprehension	Functional Reading Level
90% to 100%	Independent Reading Level
60% to 90%	Instructional Reading Level
59% or less	Frustration Reading Level

The functional reading levels for comprehension are defined below.

Independent Level. At this level, the child can read selections that have normal inflectional language patterns and can understand almost all of what he reads.

Reading in materials at this level is most likely to be enjoyable for the child.

Instructional Level.   At this level, the child can read material without undue stress or frustration and can understand enough of what he reads to make sense of the selection. The child's ability to understand what he reads can increase from instruction at this level, although reading is not particularly easy.

Frustration Level.   At this level, the child encounters many words he does not know the meaning of, concepts he does not understand, and language patterns that are unfamiliar. Often the child is not able to read the selection with normal inflectional patterns and intonation. Reading material at this level is not pleasurable, the child is incapable of answering questions related to the material.

Both aspects of the child's test performance—word recognition and comprehension—must be interpreted together in making a final assignment to appropriate instructional materials. Although this interpretation is always subjective, a few suggestions may be helpful.

At the primary reading levels, interpretation should focus mostly on word recognition on the assumption that beginning reading instruction should concentrate on decoding skills. At the intermediate and advanced reading levels, interpretation should focus primarily on comprehension, since silent-reading comprehension is of greatest importance after the child has attained basic decoding fluency.

The final interpretation of test performance should determine first whether instruction should focus on word recognition and decoding fluency or emphasize reading comprehension, and then should determine the optimum level for active instruction (usually the instructional level) and the optimum level for independent reading (usually the independent reading level). The final interpretation also includes an effort to avoid the frustration level when planning instruction or recommending library reading.

INSTRUCTIONAL PLANNING

So far, this chapter has explained how to administer and interpret an individual informal reading inventory. The traditional use of IRI's in clinics and other kinds of tutorial settings has been for individual testing. But the IRI is now being used by regular classroom teachers with entire classes of children because of its usefulness in instructional planning. This section of the chapter describes the many uses of the IRI for instructional planning in the regular classroom.

To use IRI data for instructional planning, the teacher must administer the test to every child in the classroom and arrange the results in a *rank-order list*. An actual rank-order list for a third-grade class is shown in Figure 1-3.

The rank-order list of IRI results can then be used to formulate major goals of instruction, to guide further diagnosis for specific skills, to determine the adequacy of existing instructional materials, and to plan for grouping.

Formulating Major Goals

Knowing each child's functional reading level will help you formulate major goals—that is, establish priorities for developing reading skills. A wide range of reading levels indicates the need for major categories of skill development. For instance, if a child in the fourth grade is reading at the primer or first-reader level, his most pressing need is for decoding (word recognition) instruction. His need for decoding instruction is far greater than his need for vocabulary instruction since his oral vocabulary is probably much larger than his reading vocabulary. In this case, the child's functional reading level determines the most important instructional goal.

At higher functional reading levels, the major instructional goals are quite different. For example, consider a child whose instructional reading level is sixth or seventh grade. This level represents prior mastery of virtually all phonic elements. As a result, the child probably needs no phonics instruction but may need instruction in higher-level comprehension skills, use of the library, and advanced vocabulary—especially in science, mathematics, and social studies.

Figure 1-4 shows the relationship between instructional reading levels and skill needs. Notice how the skill needs change with each advancing level.

The rank-order list and the list of related goals are then used to guide instructional planning. Such planning includes analyzing classroom materials, selecting diagnostic instruments for skills, and grouping children for instruction.

Analyzing Materials

Appropriate materials are vital. to provide for children's individual differences. The rank-order list and list of goals are useful for determining whether existing materials are adequate. You will need appropriate materials for each level represented on the rank-order list so that each child can be placed at his instructional level. You will also need materials oriented to the basic goals of instruction at each level. Finally, you will need enough material for each level and goal to sustain instruction throughout the school year.

A practical method of analyzing available materials is to construct an analysis chart, using the information from the rank-order list and the list of goals. An analysis chart has three columns, specifying (1) the number of children at each reading level, (2) the major instructional goals, and (3) the materials available to you (listed by title) to achieve these objectives. It is also helpful to estimate the useful life of the materials in classroom days and to record this figure after each title. (For instance, a second grade basal reader may

---
figure 1-3

A RANK-ORDER LIST OF IRI RESULTS

Instructional Reading Level	Children's Names
Sixth	John Chambers, Corrine Galtman, Larry Pappas
Fifth	Joni Andrews, Ann Garrett, Margaret Hawthorne, Laura Thomas, Kurt Buckridge
Fourth	Sally Anderson, James Benson, Shawna Jensen, DeAnn Jones
Third	(High Third) Alan Michaels, Ben Olean
	(Low Third) Robert DeForrest, Lisa Miles, Don Patrick, Mary Rudelsky, Pam McAdams, Julie Ralsey
Second	Brad Evans, Mark Shipley, Kenny Petersen
	(Low Second) Files Shipman, David Sampson
First	Mike Goines
Primer	David McCann

---
figure 1-4

FUNCTIONAL READING LEVELS AND MAJOR GOALS

Instructional Reading Level	Major Goals Appropriate for This Level
Primer	Visual Discrimination Auditory Discrimination Letter Sounds Vocabulary
Level One	Sight Words Basic Phonic Patterns Simplest Structural Patterns Comprehension of Literal Meaning Vocabulary

Level Two	Sight Words
	Advanced Phonic Patterns
	Intermediate Structural Patterns
	Oral Decoding Fluency
	Comprehension: Recall, Summarization, Organization
	Vocabulary
Level Three	All Phonic Patterns
	Advanced Structural Patterns
	Oral Decoding Fluency
	Oral Interpretation
	Beginning Dictionary Skills
	Comprehension: Recall, Summarization, Organization, and Interpretation
	Vocabulary
Level Four	Comprehension: Recall, Summarization, Organization, Interpretation, and Evaluation
	Mathematics, Social Studies, and Science Reading
	Vocabulary
Level Five	Comprehension: Mathematics, Social Studies, and Science Reading
	Adjusting Reading Rates
	Library Reporting Skills
	Vocabulary
Level Six	Comprehension: All Categories
	Content-Area Reading
	Report Writing and Use of Sources
	Expanding Interests
	Vocabulary

have a useful life of about forty days. Thus, you would enter (40) after the title on the analysis chart.) A sample analysis chart is shown in Figure 1-5.

The materials analysis chart can reveal whether or not your classroom materials will provide adequately for children's individual differences throughout the school year. If your materials are inadequate, the chart will indicate the types of materials you need to fulfill a well-defined goal. If appropriate materials are not available within the school district, the analysis chart is an objective means of communicating specific needs to those responsible for buying instructional materials for the schools.

Planning Skill Diagnosis

The combined rank-order list and list of goals also imply the skill diagnosis that remains to be done. For example, the rank-order list may indicate that five children have an instructional level equivalent to a first reader. The list of goals shows that phonics instruction

is appropriate for this level. The next logical step would be to do further testing to determine which phonics elements each child does or does not know in order to plan instruction. At a higher level, the rank-order list may indicate that twelve children have an instructional level equivalent to a fourth-grade reader. The list of goals shows that reading instruction in the content areas is a major goal. The next step would be to do further testing to determine the kind of instruction each child needs in order to read social studies, mathematics, or science materials with greater understanding. In each case, using the rank-order list and list of goals has suggested the types of diagnosis needed and has saved time by indicating the type of diagnosis that is *not* needed.

Grouping

Because the rank-order list of IRI results specifies the names of children who read on the same functional reading level—that is, children who share common

─────── figure 1-5 ───

ANALYSIS CHART OF READING MATERIALS

Number of Children by Reading Level	Major Goals	Suitable Materials
Sixth G.E.	Comprehension Report Writing Content-Area Reading	(List by Title)
Fifth G.E.	Comprehension Reading Rate Library Skills	
Fourth G.E.	Comprehension Vocabulary Content-Area Reading	
Third G.E.	Advanced Word Recognition Decoding Fluency Oral Interpretation Basic Comprehension	
Second G.E.	Intermediate Word Recognition Decoding Fluency Basic Comprehension	
First G.E.	Sight Words Beginning Word Recognition	

G.E. = Grade Equivalent

───

goals and thus may benefit from similar materials and similar types of teacher instruction—it is a useful device for grouping children for reading instruction. However, the rank-order list may often indicate that more groups are needed than you alone can handle. A practical solution that will provide for the full range of reading levels, allow children upward mobility when they show progress, and conserve teacher time and energy is to become partners with another compatible teacher.

Administer IRI's to all of the children in both classrooms and make a combined rank-order list and list of goals. Then decide how many reading groups each of you is able to manage (most teachers can handle two or three groups). Divide the combined classes into six levels based on the IRI results, and assign three different levels to each teacher.

For example, the rank-order list for two combined fourth-grade classes (Figure 1-6) indicates the number of children at each functional reading level.

Each teacher becomes responsible for several groups. You may assume responsibility for levels 1, 4, and 6; your partner may teach levels 2, 3, and 5. During the reading period, some children from your partner's class would come to your room for instruction in reading and other children in your class would go to your teaching partner's room for instruction.

This plan for grouping has the advantage of providing instruction to meet the full range of reading levels. Further, the division of responsibility means that neither teacher is seriously overloaded. From the child's standpoint, the advantages are even greater. The groups will be small enough so that all children receive a fair share of the teacher's attention. Since the groups in both classrooms are composed of children at varying levels of reading ability, neither room can be labeled the "dumb" room or the "smart" room. Finally, such grouping offers children the opportunity for promotion from one group to the next based on future IRI performance and teacher judgment.

figure 1-6 ———————————————————

*RANK-ORDER LIST FOR TWO COMBINED
FOURTH-GRADE CLASSES*

Level	Number of Children	Teacher
6	4	You
5	6	Partner
4	18	You
3	12	Partner
2	10	Partner
1	6	You

Parent-Teacher Conferences

An additional advantage of using the IRI for grouping is facilitated communication between teacher and parents. Parents are often concerned about the reading group their child is in, wanting their offspring to be in the highest group possible. Explaining to parents how the IRI is used for grouping will reassure them that their child is receiving the kind of instruction he needs. Parents will also be reassured to know that their child has the opportunity to advance to another group as soon as he shows sufficient progress on another IRI.

The IRI has many clear advantages. It provides a rational basis for setting goals, grouping, analyzing materials, diagnosing skills, and communicating with parents. But the vexing question is when can it be given? How can the teacher responsible for thirty children find time to administer an IRI to each child?

FINDING TIME

Administering an IRI requires about twenty minutes. Where, you may ask, do I get that much time for each child? Here are some possibilities.

1. Provide very simple independent activities for the class to do for twenty minutes, twice a day. Tell the children that they must be quiet so that you can work with one child. Administer one IRI during each period.

2. Ask one child to come to school early each day so that you can listen to him read. Ask another child to stay after school for the same purpose.

3. If you have a visiting art, music, or P.E. teacher, test one child during each of these special activities.

4. Test one child during recess.

5. If you have a resource teacher, remedial reading teacher, or other helping teacher in the building, ask for help in administering IRI's.

6. Plan a lengthy afternoon art project and ask two or three mothers to come in to supervise. Use the time to give several IRI's.

As you have probably recognized, the magical ingredient is nothing more than fierce determination. Remember that the IRI results have great potential for heading off learning problems and planning high-quality instruction. Placing children at their optimum level for reading instruction aids learning and helps prevent discipline problems. Using the IRI results to formulate instructional goals gives you a feeling of assurance and professionalism. Applying the results to grouping—especially in partnership with another teacher—saves both teachers time and energy. And finally, using the results to communicate effectively with parents can help establish a rapport between parents and teacher—those who are most concerned that all children receive the best education possible. In John Gardner's words, "Who ever said it would be easy?"[1]

AN APPLICATION EXERCISE

Up to now, you have been reading about the informal reading inventory. You have learned how to administer one, how to process the resulting data, and how to use the results for instruction. To consolidate these skills, perform the following application exercise:

1. Administer IRI's to several children of different ages and abilities.

2. Determine each child's instructional, independent, and frustration reading levels.

3. Construct a rank-order list of IRI results.

4. Formulate major goals for each reading level represented on the rank-order list.

5. Analyze the adequacy of the reading materials in a single classroom in relation to the rank-order list and the list of goals.

6. If possible, select and use a follow-up test to diagnose the specific skills related to the child's instructional level.

7. Explain the IRI procedures and results to each child's parents.

———————————————————

[1]John W. Gardner, *Excellence* (New York: Harper & Row, 1961).

VISION AND VISUAL DISCRIMINATION

will enable you to

1. Identify children who need a complete eye examination by using a checklist of symptoms of visual difficulty and by interpreting the results of a binocular visual-screening test

2. Diagnose children's specific difficulties in discriminating letter shapes within whole words

3. Teach visual discrimination of letter shapes

David Seymour is an advantaged child. His father manages the local Save-U Drugstore, the largest, newest one in town. David has a room of his own in a beautiful new home. He has had many other advantages as well, such as trips to the zoo, to museums, and to Disneyland. David's parents care about him very much and have talked to him constantly, explaining the reasons and the inner workings of all kinds of things. As a result, David's test scores, wide range of interests, and oral language vocabulary all indicate above-average intelligence.

But David is a nonreader. This problem causes anguish for his mother and father, who have high aspirations for their son. They blame most of it on his first-grade teacher, who was strict and demanding. In their opinion, she hadn't really liked David or been patient with him. In contrast, the second-grade teacher had showered David with affection in the belief that his problem of nonreading was emotional. David's parents have done what they could—encouraged him, provided many books for him, and had him examined by a pediatrician and an ophthalmologist. The only result is a new pair of glasses, which don't seem to make much difference in his reading.

David's reading problem hangs on. He is a wild word-guesser and a surrealistic speller. And his handwriting is atrocious. To top it off, he says he doesn't care.

How would you analyze David's problem? _____

_____

_____

What would you do about it? _____

_____

_____

_____

Children like David, who are advantaged and obviously bright, sometimes fail to profit from reading instruction for no apparent reason. This problem confounds reading teachers, parents, and children. Many theories have been formulated to account for it. Most theories about learning disabilities like David's are related to subtle, neurological defects that prevent the child from seeing letters and words as other children see them, and thus prevent them from learning to read. Such children are called *dyslexic, minimally brain-damaged,* or *strephosymbolic* (word-blind). Various methods are used to treat the condition. Some optometrists use visual exercises. Specialists in learning disabilities have developed physical exercise programs to increase visual interpretive abilities through developing the central nervous system. Still others have developed special workbooks to improve eye-hand coordination. None of these remedial methods has produced conclusive or consistent results in research studies.

There is considerable evidence that some children do, indeed, have visual problems that inhibit their reading. Studies by ophthalmologists, optometrists, and reading specialists show that poor readers have a much higher incidence of visual problems than do good readers. It is clearly worthwhile for you to know enough about vision and visual interpretation to offer children like David the best help available, consistent with what is known and what can be diagnosed and treated by teachers. For this reason, this chapter presents basic information about visual problems, some visual-screening methods, a diagnostic method for visual discrimination, and a method for teaching visual discrimination.

VISION

As a reading teacher, you need to know some things about the anatomy of the eye and how it functions. To begin with, the eye is a complex receptor organ. It is a ball-like structure filled with a gelatinous substance (the vitreous humor) and encased by a tough membrane. At the front of the eyeball is an aper-

DIAGRAM OF EYE

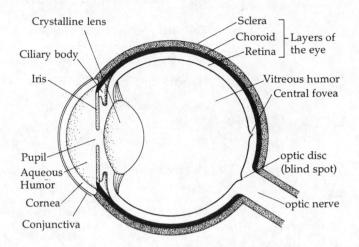

ture (the pupil) and a lens. The amount of light admitted into the eye is controlled by the iris. The point of focus is controlled by muscles that expand and contract the lens (a process called "accommodation"). Both operations are controlled by the brain.

At the back of the eyeball is a point of focus, called the retina, for the light admitted into the eye. The retina contains a light-sensitive layer of rods and cones that translate light impulses into nerve impulses. A series of nerves then transmit these impulses to the brain.

There are six muscular strands attached to the sides of each eyeball. These muscular strands aim the eyeball in accordance with instructions received from the brain.

The eye and brain are thus interdependent organs. The eye receives light, translates light into neurological impulses, and sends the impulses to the brain. At the same time, the brain controls the eye— regulating the amount of light that enters, aiming the eyes, and coordinating their movements. In addition, the brain gives the nerve impulses their meaning. It is important to remember that we do not see just with our eyes. In fact, it is more accurate to say that we "see" with our brain.

Now consider what happens when a child reads:

When a child looks at a word, he aims both eyes at it (convergence), and his lenses bulge enough to bring it into focus (accommodation). His eyes move along the line in jumps and pauses, each jump ending in a new fixation. This requires very exact coordination of both convergence and accommodation. Failure to do this accurately accounts for many errors.[1]

Amazingly, most children make the necessary adjustments and interpretations precisely enough to learn to read. But sometimes things go wrong. For example, the eyes may not focus light exactly on the retina; the point of focus may fall short (nearsightedness) or long (farsightedness). The cornea may be distorted and focus a distorted image on the retina (astigmatism). The eyes may not be mates; one may be more or less nearsighted or farsighted. Or each eye may have a different defect: sometimes one eye is nearsighted and the other is farsighted. Sometimes the vision from one eye is suppressed by the brain. The eyes may not work well together. In extreme cases, this is called "cockeyedness" or "crosseyedness" and is very apparent. In less extreme cases, the eyes may look normal but not coordinate well enough to produce a single, fused image.

Visual defects of the kinds just described are more common among children who have reading difficulties than among those who read well. Eames studied the incidence of visual problems among 3,500 school children in Boston. Half of the children studied were reading failures and the other half were a random group of schoolchildren. Eames reports the following incidence (in percentages) of visual problems for both groups.

---

[1]Thomas J. Eames, "Visual Handicaps to Reading," *Journal of Education* 141, no. 3 (1959): 3–4.

—————— figure 2-1 ——

VISUAL PROBLEMS AMONG SCHOOL CHILDREN

Problem	Definition	All Children	Reading Failures
Myopia	Nearsightedness	(similar)→	4%
Hypermetropia	Farsightedness	12%	43%
Astigmatism	Corneal defect	(similar)→	5%
Fusion	Difficulty in obtaining a single image	18%	22%
Heterophoria	Lack of coordination between eyes	28%	37%

Compiled from Eames, "Visual Handicaps to Reading," *Journal of Education* 141 (1959): 6–15.

According to Eames, the visual defects that occur most often among reading failures are the same ones that interfere most with reading. For example, many poor readers are farsighted. Although they may be able to see things at close range, they must strain to bring their vision into focus. This constant straining is tiring and children soon turn their attention to something farther away, perhaps gazing out the classroom window to allow their eyes to rest. While this inattention may be unconscious on the child's part, the teacher might interpret this behavior as daydreaming rather than as a symptom of visual impairment.

Heterophoria, or lack of coordination between both eyes, is another common problem. Reading requires that both eyes focus together to produce a clear, single image. But a child with heterophoria may be able to coordinate both eyes only with considerable effort. Generally, such children can do this briefly but soon get tired. With fatigue, their eyes begin to lose coordination and these children may begin to make errors such as substitutions, omissions, regressions, and loss of place in the text.

Detecting Visual Impairment

Many visual problems can be detected in the classroom through informed observation. The teacher can learn to identify children who have visual impairment by using the following checklist published by the American Optometric Association.

If a child's behavior indicates that he may have a visual problem, his vision should be tested. Every school should have a good procedure for testing vision—one that will identify the kinds of impairments that interfere most with reading, such as hypermetropia (farsightedness), heterophoria (lack of coordination), and fusion defects. The most common visual-screening test, the Snellen, is inadequate. Since the Snellen test is given at a distance of twenty feet and not at the reading distance, it does not identify children who are farsighted. Further, because the Snellen tests the vision of each eye separately, it does not test how both eyes work together as mates, thus missing such visual defects as heterophoria.

A binocular visual-screening test given with a special desk-top testing machine will identify many children who have the kinds of visual defects that interfere most with reading. The Keystone Visual Survey Test, for example, is one machine of this type (see illustration).

The binocular visual-screening test is administered individually from a manual that specifies exact procedures. Each child is given fourteen test items designed to assess the following visual abilities:

Simultaneous Vision

Vertical Posture

Lateral Posture

Fusion

Usable Vision, Both Eyes ⎫

Usable Vision, Right Eye ⎬ **Far Point**

Usable Vision, Left Eye

Stereopsis

Color Perception ⎭

—— figure 2-2 ——

A VISION SYMPTOM CHECKLIST

THE ABC'S OF VISION DIFFICULTY

A's – APPEARANCE OF THE EYES:
Eyes crossed or turning in, out, or moving independently of each other. ____ ____

Reddened eyes, watering eyes, encrusted eyelids, frequent styes. ____ ____

B's – BEHAVIORAL INDICATIONS OF POSSIBLE VISION DIFFICULTY:
Body rigidity while looking at distant or near objects or while performing in class: ____ ____

Avoiding close work. ____ ____

Unusually short attention span or frequent daydreaming. ____ ____

Turning of head so as to use one eye only, or tilting of head to one side. ____ ____

Placing head close to book or desk when reading or writing. ____ ____

Frowning or scowling while reading, writing or doing blackboard work. ____ ____

Using unusual or fisted pencil grasp, frequently breaking pencil, and frequent rotation of paper when writing. ____ ____

Spidery, excessively sloppy, or very hard to read handwriting. ____ ____

Excessive blinking or excessive rubbing of eyes. ____ ____

Closing or covering one eye ____ ____

Dislike for tasks requiring sustained visual concentration. Nervousness, irritability, restlessness, or unusual fatigue after maintaining visual concentration. ____ ____

Losing place while reading and using finger or marker to guide eyes and keep place while reading. ____ ____

Saying the words aloud or lip reading. ____ ____

Difficulty in remembering what is read. ____ ____

Skipping words and re-reading. ____ ____

Persistent reversals after the second grade. ____ ____

Difficulty remembering, identifying and reproducing basic geometric forms. ____ ____

Difficulty with sequential concepts. ____ ____

Confusion of similar words. ____ ____

Difficulty following verbal instructions. ____ ____

Poor eye-hand coordination and unusual awkwardness including difficulty going up and down stairs, throwing or catching a ball, buttoning or unbuttoning clothing or tying shoes. ____ ____

Displaying evidence of developmental immaturity. ____ ____

Low frustration level, withdrawn, and difficulty getting along with other children. ____ ____

C's – COMPLAINTS ASSOCIATED WITH USING THE EYES:

Headaches, nausea, and dizziness. ____ ____

Burning or itching of eyes. ____ ____

Blurring of vision at any time. ____ ____

Reprinted from A Teacher's Guide to Vision Problems *by permission of the American Optometric Association.*

Lateral Posture

Fusion

Usable Vision, Both Eyes } Near Point

Usable Vision, Left Eye

Usable Vision, Right Eye

The child's responses are scored with a series of marks on the answer sheet shown below. Notice the set of heavy black lines on the right side of the scoring sheet. These lines indicate the boundaries of relatively normal vision. If all the child's scores are inside the heavy black lines, he probably has normal vision. If the child has one or more responses outside the heavy black lines, he may have a visual impairment that should be further diagnosed and treated by an ophthalmologist (an eye specialist).

The child who has been identified as having visual impairment needs special attention in the classroom until the condition can be further diagnosed and treated by a specialist. The following guidelines will help.

1. If the child is nearsighted, seat him close to the chalkboard. Also, allow him to hold his book closer to his face, since he can often bring print into focus this way.

A TELEBINOCULAR VISUAL-SCREENING DEVICE

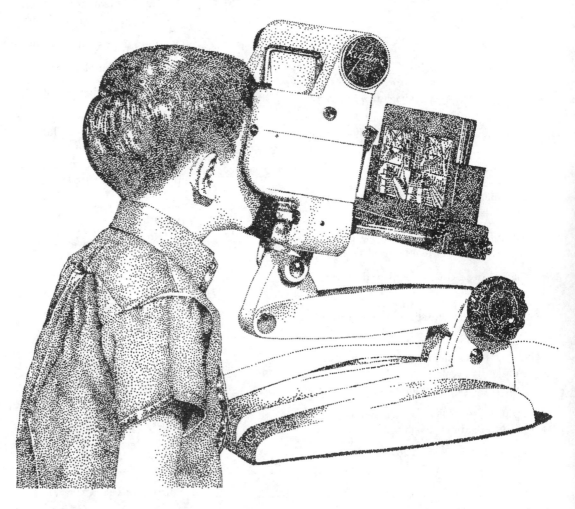

Courtesy of Mast/Keystone, Keystone View Division, Davenport, Iowa.

KEYSTONE

School Vision Screening

FOR USE WITH THE KEYSTONE TELEBINOCULAR
SCHOOL SURVEY CUMULATIVE RECORD FORM NO. 5-B
(CATALOG ORDER NO. 5522-B)

Name _____ Sex _____
School _____ City _____
Grade _____ Room _____ Teacher _____
Date of birth _____ Date of test _____

Wearing glasses? Yes: For reading only _____; both _____. No. _____
for distance only _____
Snellen Standard (if desired)
With glasses: RE _____ LE _____
Without glasses: RE _____ LE _____

Examined by: _____

RAPID VISION SCREENING TESTS

	Pass	Fail

DISTANT VISION TESTS

1A. Dog should be seen jumping over pig
The 4 blocks should be seen merged into 3

2A. Balloon No. 2 is farthest away
Balloon No. 5 is closest
Balloon 2 is red: balloon 5 is green (Training only)
Letters in Block A: D C Z P T
Letters in Block B: Z P D T C *
Letters in Block C: L D T C Z *

NEAR VISION TESTS (16 INCHES)

3A. Yellow line should pass through white square
The 4 balls should be merged into 3

4A. Letters in Block A: L O Z P C (Training only)
Letters in Block B: T Z O D L *
Letters in Block C: O P T D C *

Passing score: at least 4 letters

Failure on any test above indicates need for full test at right.

COMPREHENSIVE TEST BATTERY: QUESTIONS

1. What do you see?
2. Does the yellow line go through, above, or below the red ball?
3. To what number, or between what numbers, does the arrow point?
4. How many balls do you see?
4½. In each signboard there are five diamonds (point). In one diamond is a dot. (point to first signboard, show dot in the left diamond.) Ask: Where is the dot in Nos. 2, 3, 4, 5, etc? *Tests 5 and 6 are the same as No. 4½. Ask Where is the dot?*
7. (Point to the top line of symbols and name each one. Show by pointing that the cross stands out in 3-D.) Ask: Which symbol stands out in each of the next lines?
8. What number is in the upper circle? The lower left? The lower right? (*Test 9 is the same as Test 8.*)
10. To what number, or between what numbers, does the arrow point?
12. How many balls do you see?
12. In the three circles in the center (point) you see black crossed lines, black dots, and solid gray. Starting with No. 1 of the outer circles, you see black dots. No. 2 has black lines. What do you see in No. 3? Go as far as you can. *Tests 13 and 14 are the same as 12:* Name what you see in each of the circles.

Record Form Table

FAR POINT TESTS

TEST	LEFT EYE ONLY	RIGHT EYE ONLY	UNSATISFACTORY (Underconvergence and/or low usable vision)	RE-TEST AREA	EXPECTED RESPONSE	RE-TEST AREA	UNSATISFACTORY (Overconvergence)
1 (DB-10A) Simultaneous Vision							
2 Vertical Posture	only	only	15 14 13 12	11	10	7	6 5 4 3 2 1
3 Lateral Posture	Arrow only	Numbers only	15 14 13 12	11	10	7	Close ... Far apart
4 (DB-4K) Fusion	only	only	Far apart ... Close				Close ... Far apart
4½ (DB-1D) Usable Vision Both Eyes			1 49% 2 70% 3 84% 4 88% 5 92%	6 96%	7 98% 8 100% 9 103% 10 105%		
5 (DB-1D) Usable Vision, Right Eye		No Dots Seen Unless Left Eye Is Occluded	1 49% 2 70% 3 84% 4 88% 5 92%	6 96%	7 98% 8 100% 9 103% 10 105%		
6 (DB-2D) Usable Vision Left Eye	NO Dots Seen Unless Right Eye Is Occluded		1 49% 2 70% 3 84% 4 88% 5 92%	6 96%	7 98% 8 100% 9 103% 10 105%		
7 (DB-6D) Stereopsis	+ only	only •	+ * * +	*	+		

NEAR POINT TESTS

TEST	LEFT EYE ONLY	RIGHT EYE ONLY	UNSATISFACTORY (Underconvergence and/or low usable vision)	RE-TEST AREA	EXPECTED RESPONSE	RE-TEST AREA	UNSATISFACTORY (Overconvergence)
8 (DB-13A) Color Perception	Top 32	Left 79 / Right 23	NONE CORRECT	1 Out of 3	2 out of 3	ALL CORRECT	
9 (DB-14A) Color Perception	Top 63	Left 92 / Right 56	NONE CORRECT	1 Out of 3	2 out of 3	ALL CORRECT	
10 (DB-9B) Lateral Posture	Arrow only	Numbers only	10 9 8	7	6	3	5 4
11 (DB-5K) Fusion	only	only	Far apart ... Close				Close ... Far apart
12 (DB-15) Usable Vision Both Eyes	1 D 10%	2 L 20% 3 D 30% 4 L 40%	5 L 50% 6 D 60% 7 D 70% 8 L 80% 9 D 70% 10 D 70% 11 G 80% 12 L 80%	13 L 90% 14 L 90%	15 D 100% 16 L 100% 17 L 100% 18 L 102% 19 D 102% 20 D 103% 21 L 105% 22 L 105%		
13 (DB-16) Usable Vision Right Eye	1 D 10%	2 L 20% 3 D 30% 4 L 40%	5 D 50% 6 D 60% 7 L 70% 8 L 80% 9 D 70% 10 D 70% 11 G 80% 12 L 80%	13 L 90% 14 L 90%	15 D 100% 16 L 100% 17 L 100% 18 L 102% 19 G 102% 20 D 103% 21 L 105% 22 L 105%		
14 (DB-17) Usable Vision Left Eye	1 L 10%	2 L 20% 3 D 30% 4 D 40%	5 L 50% 6 D 60% 7 L 70% 8 D 80% 9 D 70% 10 L 70% 11 G 80% 12 L 80%	13 G 90% 14 L 90%	15 D 100% 16 L 100% 17 L 100% 18 L 102% 19 G 102% 20 L 103% 21 L 105% 22 L 105%		

2.   If the child is farsighted, reduce your demands for close work markedly. Alternate assignments and activities so that the child does near-point work for a short time and then does far-point work, such as chalkboard exercises, which will allow his eyes to function at a more comfortable distance.

3.   If the child has more complex difficulties, discontinue assignments requiring any close, near-point discriminations until he has been examined by an eye doctor.

4.   Many children, especially those with marked visual defects, will benefit by adequate, glare-free lighting in the classroom, from texts with plain, bold letters and wide line spacing, printed on a matte surface.

5.   Be aware of where you stand when you teach. Stand in front of a nonglare surface to talk to children. If you stand in front of a window when addressing the class, when children turn to look at you their eyes will adjust to the harsh light. When they turn again to their books or writing, their eyes must strain to readjust rapidly.

Children who already wear glasses should also be observed closely. There is a great temptation to think that children with glasses have been adequately cared for—they have been examined by a professional, received appropriate treatment, and are therefore cured. This is a faulty assumption for several reasons. First, glasses may improve usable vision by focusing light more directly on the retina, but they do not "cure" anything. For example, they do not increase the eye's sensitivity to light or cure eye diseases. Second, young children's eye defects are very hard to diagnose. A first grader may be wearing glasses that were prescribed at the age of four or five. The child's responses to the eye doctor's questions may have been unstable and difficult to interpret, resulting in a less-than-perfect correction. Third, the child's eyes may have changed through maturation. For all these reasons, children with glasses should be watched and tested for visual difficulties just as carefully as children who do not wear glasses.

Visual acuity, the subject of this chapter to this point, is only part of the problem. Seeing is an interpretive act. A child may see letters on paper but not notice the significant differences between them. Therefore, diagnosis and instruction for visual discrimination of letters is also necessary.

VISUAL DISCRIMINATION

To begin learning to read, a child must be able to tell the difference between letters. He must notice that the upright line on *h*, for example, is higher than the similar line on *n*. He must notice also that the oval on *b*

is on the right side, and that the oval on *d* is on the left side. He must recognize that these are the critical differences used to distinguish between letters. To an adult reader, this may sound trivial. Why wouldn't the child recognize these differences as being important? The answer is that for a child, small differences in shape, size, and direction are seldom used to distinguish between various objects.

Dogs, for example, come in various configurations of color, size, shape, and distinguishing features. But the child recognizes by school age that "a dog is a dog," in spite of the differences. Directionality seldom makes a difference, either. Toy trucks are identified as such in spite of the direction they may be facing. A toy truck is still a toy truck whether it is viewed from the left or the right. Consequently, letter discrimination is quite different from the kinds of discriminations the child has made in the past. In addition, children with visual impairment may have trouble with visual tasks that other children perform easily. Or, children whose visual defects have recently been corrected with glasses may need help in recognizing significant differences in letter shapes that they were incapable of seeing before. In all these cases—whether with beginning readers, poor readers, or visually impaired readers—diagnosis and instruction for visual discrimination may be of first importance.

Diagnosing Visual Discrimination Skills

Begin diagnosing visual discrimination by asking the child to identify likenesses and differences of letters in whole words. For example, you may present the child with the following item:

Directions: Look at the first word in this list. Circle each word that begins with the same letter as the word at the top of the list.

   time

   file

   happy

   list

   tip

   riddle

   topping

If the child circles the words *tip* and *topping*, you may assume that he can discriminate between words beginning with initial consonant *t* and other words beginning with letters that look much the same. In this case, he needs no instruction for visual discrimination of initial consonant *t*. If he circles other words in the list, indicating confusion over likenesses and differences in very similar letters, he probably does need instruction for visual discrimination of initial consonant *t*.

This same procedure can be used to diagnose the child's ability to visually discriminate other letters within whole words. A diagnostic instrument for use in planning instruction should include an item for each of the hardest visual discrimination tasks a child is asked to make while reading. These most difficult discriminations are those between letters having similar features, such as the following:

b-d

g-p-q

m-n-u-w

n-h-k

l-t-f

a-o-c-u

Figure 2-3 is a model instrument for diagnosing visual discrimination of these letter combinations.

Since a child must be able to tell the differences between letter shapes to read similar words, any errors he makes on this test are important. The criterion for each skill item is 100% accuracy. If the child makes any errors, he probably needs instruction in visual discrimination.

Figure 2-4 is useful for recording children's errors on this test.

The grid lists each visual discrimination skill. Check the child's answer sheet to determine the kinds of errors he is making and mark the grid with the following system:

Mark	Meaning
0	Scored perfectly on the test. No instruction needed.
/	At least one error on an item of this type. Instruction is needed.
X	Instruction has been given for this skill. The child has now attained mastery.

Teaching Visual Discrimination

Children who have difficulty discriminating between letters can be helped through active teaching and follow-up activities. Active teaching is directed toward the specific letter discriminations the child cannot make. For example, if the child's performance

on the diagnostic inventory indicates that he cannot discriminate initial consonant *d* from similar letters, you might plan your instruction for that specific skill. The alternative method is to instruct for visual discrimination generally, having the child make discriminations with geometric forms, common objects, mazes, and the like in the hope that discriminating among such things will enable the child to discriminate letter shapes. It could happen. But the best evidence to date supports the efficacy of practice on the specific letters the child must learn to discriminate.

Instruction for visual discrimination follows certain principles. First, children should begin by making easy visual discriminations, then do moderately difficult discriminations, and finally advance to difficult discriminations. For example, if a child cannot discriminate initial *d* from similar letters, begin by presenting him with some easy discriminations. The contrast between *b* and *t* is quite simple. Begin by writing word-pairs that contrast *b* and *t*.

ball	bin	tame
tin	bail	bag

Ask the child if each of these word-pairs begins with the same or a different letter. If he responds correctly, present a series of word-pairs with beginning letters that are more alike. The *b* and *h* contrast is an example.

bin	belt	halt	ham
hinge	boat	bit	bomb

Again, ask the child if these words begin with the same or a different letter. If he responds correctly, go on to the most difficult contrast, *b* and *d*.

ball	dig	bat	bit
dill	bill	but	bin

Again, ask the child to tell whether the words begin with the same or a different letter. If he responds correctly, he has learned to make the discrimination you have been trying to teach. In this event, continue practice on this skill for a brief time during subsequent lessons to ensure mastery. Then go on to some new skill he still needs to learn.

Children sometimes make errors during this procedure. For example, you may present the following word-pairs:

bin	belt	halt	ham
hinge	bolt	bit	bomb

The child may say that the first word-pair is the same. To help him, do two things. First, have him trace over the two letter shapes, *b* and *h*, with his finger. Second, ask him to describe the similarities and differences in the shapes of the two letters. If he has difficulty, prompt him. Then ask him again to tell if the beginning letters are alike or different. Use the same correction procedure whenever the child has difficulty.

After active instruction of this type, you may wish to have the child do a follow-up activity for visual discrimination. Some of the best activities for this purpose include dot-to-dot tracing of letter shapes, tracing letter shapes in a tray of soft white sand, tracing

---

—— figure 2-3 ——

A VISUAL DISCRIMINATION DIAGNOSTIC TEST

Directions: Look at the first word in each list. Notice the underlined letter or letters. Circle each word in the following list that has the same letter in the same place. (The letter may be at the beginning, middle, or end of the word.)

BEGINNING LETTERS

band	**grin**	**made**	**noise**	**fist**
doll	grow	notch	hope	till
point	point	wild	nickle	lip
dive	quick	many	kosher	froze
grow	drop	ugly	nice	fit
build	ghost	notice	mice	tick

FINAL LETTERS

lead	**drop**	**flaw**	**black**	**scat**
drag	frog	paw	blah	half
crab	clip	slam	tack	hat
stop	slop	grin	calf	until
clod	crib	strum	sack	sheriff
club	dread	draw	tall	slit

MIDDLE LETTERS

blat	**trunk**	**bead**
brat	brat	leap
shun	thud	toad
crop	find	found
lick	trudge	team
drat	prance	field

sandpaper letters on wood squares, and tracing letter shapes on grooved, wooden alphabet blocks made for this purpose. Any of these activities may help the child form a clearer mental image of letter shapes.

Once you have become familiar with all of the techniques discussed in this chapter—visual screening, diagnosing visual discrimination skills, and teaching visual discrimination skills—you will be able to help many children like David Seymour, whose problem was described at the beginning of this chapter.

You will be able to determine whether children with visual problems need a complete eye examination by an eye doctor; you will be able to diagnose children's abilities to do the most important visual discrimination tasks needed for reading. And you will have the teaching skills necessary to help any child who confuses letter shapes. Of course, you cannot cure basic neurological defects, but your efforts may lessen a child's difficulties with reading and improve his chances for success in school.

--- figure 2-4 ---

A DIAGNOSTIC GRID

BEGINNING LETTERS

		m	n	
b	q	n	h	f
d	b	w	m	t
g	d	u	k	l

names

1. _____

2. _____

3. _____

FINAL LETTERS

d	p		k	
q	q	w	h	t
b	b	m	i	f
p	d	n	f	l

names

1. _____

2. _____

3. _____

MIDDLE LETTERS

a		ea
u	u	oa
o	a	ou
c	i	ie

names

1. _____

2. _____

3. _____

AN APPLICATION EXERCISE Up to now, you have been reading about diagnosis and correction of vision and visual discrimination difficulties. But there is a vast difference between reading about anything and actually learning to do it. To consolidate your knowledge and skills, do the following application exercise:

1. Identify a child who may have visual problems by using the checklist of symptoms of the visual difficulty.

2. Review the child's school health record for information about his or her vision.

3. Have the child's vision tested with a binocular visual-screening device. If no trained person is available to give the test, test the child yourself by following the directions in the manual that accompanies the machine.

4. Administer the visual discrimination diagnostic test included in this chapter and chart the results.

5. Teach the child to discriminate between any letter shapes that confuse him by using the teaching method described.

HEARING AND AUDITORY DISCRIMINATION

will enable you to

1. Identify children who need a complete hearing examination

2. Interpret the results of an audiogram

3. Diagnose children's specific difficulties with auditory discrimination

4. Teach auditory discrimination of letter sounds

Michelle Wilson often goes unnoticed. She weighs twenty pounds less than her fifth-grade classmates even though she is slightly taller than average. Her face is thin and pointed and her skin looks pale and drawn. Although Michelle enters into active games, she tires quickly and soon drops out.

She never starts a conversation, especially with her teacher, and won't talk in class discussions even when she understands the topic. When she must speak, her voice is so quiet she is usually asked to repeat herself.

Michelle is absent often. Each absence is explained by a note about a cold, a sore throat, or an earache. This all seems eminently believable since she has a perpetually plugged nose in class.

Michelle's schoolwork is only fair. Her reading scores are near the thirtieth percentile, indicating that she is probably a year behind grade level. Her I.Q. scores show a diminishing pattern in the average range—103 in kindergarten, 97 in first grade, and 91 in third grade. In basic achievement areas, she is strongest in math and science. But her scores plummet on spelling. Her daily work in spelling confirms this—a strange mixture of consistency and surprising mistakes on easy words.

Her mother thinks she should be doing better in school than she is, particularly in the language arts.

How would you analyze the problem? _____

_____

_____

_____

What would you do about it? _____

_____

_____

_____

_____

_____

Michelle obviously has more than one problem that interferes with her progress in school. She has frequent upper-respiratory illnesses. She is socially withdrawn and painfully shy. Although all of these problems are significant, they may be the accompanying signs of a marked hearing loss—a condition that is almost certain to interfere with academic achievement.

To help children like Michelle, the teacher must first understand some essential facts about hearing loss and auditory discrimination. This chapter presents basic information about hearing impairment, describes some hearing screening and testing procedures, and offers a method for diagnosing and teaching auditory discrimination.

HEARING

The Hearing Mechanism

Let's begin with a brief overview of the anatomy and physiology of the hearing mechanism. First, it is useful to consider the hearing mechanism in three parts: the outer ear, the middle ear, and the inner ear (see the illustration below). The outer ear includes the visible portion, or auricle, and the external canal leading to the eardrum. The auricle serves to deflect sound into the external canal, a relatively minor role. The external canal funnels sound to the eardrum.

THE HEARING MECHANISM

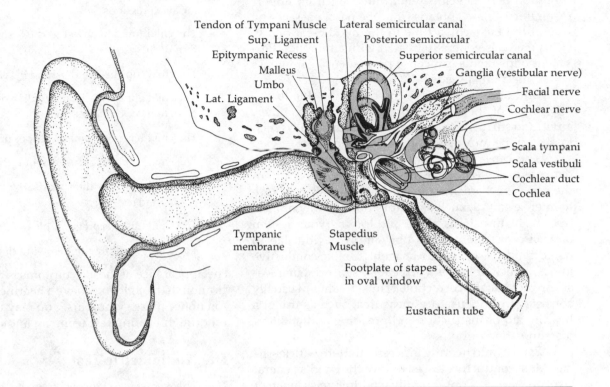

Tendon of Tympani Muscle
Sup. Ligament
Epitympanic Recess
Malleus
Umbo
Lat. Ligament

Lateral semicircular canal
Posterior semicircular
Superior semicircular canal
Ganglia (vestibular nerve)
Facial nerve
Cochlear nerve
Scala tympani
Scala vestibuli
Cochlear duct
Cochlea

Tympanic membrane
Stapedius Muscle
Footplate of stapes in oval window
Eustachian tube

The middle ear includes the eardrum and three tiny bones that transmit sound to the inner ear. The eardrum vibrates in sympathy with incoming sounds. The tiny bones—called the hammer, anvil, and stirrup—form a bridge to relay these vibrations to the inner ear. The cavity of the middle ear is connected to the back part of the throat by means of the Eustachian tube. The Eustachian tube provides a pathway for air to enter into the space behind the eardrum so that air pressure is equal on both sides of the eardrum.

The inner ear is an intricate system of tiny passageways—the labyrinth—deep within the temporal bone of the skull. The inner ear includes a number of vital mechanisms that are encased in bone and surrounded by fluid. The hearing part of the inner ear is called the cochlea. The balance apparatus of the inner ear is called the vestibular apparatus. Within the cochlea is the sensory end-organ of hearing called the organ of Corti, which translates vibrations to nerve impulses and connects to the auditory nerve in the brain. The auditory nerve is connected to the brain stem and ultimately to the cerebral cortex.

Even from this oversimplified description, we can see that there is a series of delicate and vital mechanisms that must operate perfectly to result in normal hearing. There are also a number of things that can malfunction, resulting in impaired hearing or impaired auditory discrimination.

Hearing impairments are usually classified as *conductive, sensorineural,* or *mixed. Conductive* impairments occur in the outer or middle ear. Something impedes the normal transmission of sound to the inner ear. This obstruction may be due to wax, a foreign object, or disruption of the middle-ear mechanisms. *Sensorineural* impairment occurs when the inner-ear mechanisms, auditory nerve, or brain does not respond to the signals received. *Mixed* losses include both conductive and sensorineural elements. It is important to determine whether a hearing impairment is conductive or sensorineural because each type of loss requires a different treatment. Conductive losses can often be reduced or corrected medically, whereas neural losses often cannot be corrected, so compensatory steps are necessary.

As just mentioned, there are several types of conductive impairments. If the external canal is simply blocked with wax or some other material, a physician can clean the canal or remove the blockage. Other conductive losses may be traced to the middle ear. *Otitis media* (inflammation or infection of the middle-ear cavity) is the most common cause of hearing loss. This condition may develop when infection from upper-respiratory illness spreads from the nasal passages by way of the Eustachian tube to the middle-ear cavity. Otitis media is generally treated with antibiotics. Persistent otitis media can cause permanent hearing loss when infection spreads.

Still other conductive losses can be due to deterioration of the bone composition of the hammer, anvil, and stirrup in the middle ear. Occasionally, such losses can be improved through surgery.

The cause of sensorineural impairment can be damage to the inner ear through injury. More often, the nerve mechanisms are damaged through exposure to intense sound, such as factory noise or loud music. Specific malfunctions of the auditory nervous system often are not identifiable but simply attributable to heredity, disease, or a toxic agent. Unlike conductive losses, which are often correctible, sensorineural losses are not usually correctible. Thus, treatment usually consists of compensatory measures, such as use of a hearing aid or instruction in lipreading and auditory discrimination or both.

Even a mild hearing loss can interfere with learning. Most conductive losses reduce the child's general level of hearing. Consequently, children miss much of what the teacher and their classmates say. Although they could ask others to speak louder, such hearing-impaired children may simply get used to not being able to hear. In addition, attendant problems with ear infection and other upper-respiratory infections often cause these children to miss still more through frequent absences.

Children with a sensorineural loss have additional problems. For example, neural impairment often takes place at the higher frequencies of sound. So children with a high-frequency loss miss hearing parts of words with high-frequency sounds, such as *h*, *s*, *t*, and *f*. This causes them to confuse certain words and frequently to misspell words with these sounds.

The following list of the symptoms of hearing impairment can give the knowledgeable classroom teacher the means to diagnose and help children with this serious problem.

SYMPTOMS OF HEARING IMPAIRMENT.

The child has frequent absences for upper-respiratory illnesses.

The child breathes through his mouth because of a stopped-up nose.

The child speaks very softly, too loudly, or in a monotone.

The child complains of head noises such as buzzing or ringing.

The child concentrates on your lip movements and facial expressions.

The child turns his head to catch sounds with a preferred ear.

The child cups his hand behind his ear to hear better.

The child appears to be inattentive during teacher explanations or oral discussions.

The child has poor general school progress.

The child is often confused about phonics.

The child confuses the sounds of *f, v, s, z, sh, th, t, d, p, g, k,* and *b*.

The child misinterprets simple questions.

The child has difficulty following directions.

The appearance of these symptoms is a reasonable indication that a child may have a hearing impairment. If you notice these symptoms, you may want to arrange a thorough hearing test using an audiometer.

The Audiometric Test

The *pure-tone audiometer* is the best commonly available means of determining the degree and nature of a hearing loss. This device (shown in the illustration

THE PURE-TONE AUDIOMETER

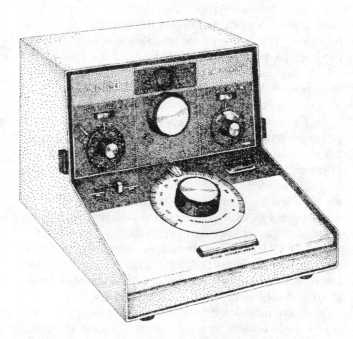

Courtesy of the Zenith Hearing Instrument Corporation.

below) emits a series of tones ranging from very low to very high at varying degrees of loudness. It is used to determine how loud each tone must be for the child to hear it.

The results of the audiometric test are plotted on a chart called an *audiogram*. Although a specialist generally gives an audiometer test, it is useful for the teacher to know how to interpret the audiogram. To begin, the audiogram lists on its horizontal axis the frequencies (in cycles per second, or *cps*) at which each sound is presented to the child. The frequencies range from 125 cps (a very low sound) to 8000 cps (a very high sound).

Audiogram Frequencies in Cycles per Second

125	250	500	1000	2000	4000	8000
					3000	6000

On the vertical axis (see Figure 3-1) the audiogram lists the decibel level (loudness)required for the child to hear each tone. The levels range from −10 (a very weak tone audible only to those with extremely good hearing) to 100 (a loud tone almost painful to those with normal hearing).

Audiogram Hearing Levels In Decibels

−10	
0	(Normal-Hearing Range)
10	
20	
30	(Mid-Loss Range)
40	
50	(Moderate-Loss Range)
60	
70	(Severe-Loss Range)
80	
90	
100	

The audiogram records the results of testing with two modes: first, air conduction (usually done with a single earphone) to determine the child's ability to hear sounds conducted through air; and second, if the air-conduction test indicates a hearing loss, bone conduction (usually done with a plastic sound vibrator), which transmits sounds through the bones of the head to the inner ear. The air-conduction marks are recorded with 0's for the right ear and X's for the left ear.

The bone-conduction results are recorded with pointers: > for the right ear and < for the left ear.

Interpreting the Results of the Test. Figure 3-1 shows an audiogram for a child with normal hearing. The air-conduction test results show a slight hearing loss on some frequencies, but all marks fall between 0 and 20 decibels. The bone-conduction test results are between 20 and 30 decibels. This also is considered normal.

When a child's hearing is impaired, the audiogram will indicate the severity of the loss. Marks between 0 and 20 decibels indicate normal hearing. Marks between 20 and 40 decibels indicate a mild hearing loss that may occasionally interfere with classroom learning. Marks between 40 and 60 decibels indicate a moderate loss that will interfere greatly with classroom learning. Marks between 60 and 100 decibels indicate a severe hearing loss.

The audiogram may show that the child has much better hearing in one ear than the other. This is apparent when the marks for each ear are widely divergent. Such information is useful for planning where the child will sit in the classroom to be able to use his best ear.

The audiogram also indicates the configuration of the loss. For example, the chart in Figure 3-2 indicates a mild loss in the lower and middle frequencies but a substantial loss in the higher frequencies. This type of loss means that the child will probably have difficulty hearing high-frequency sounds such as *f*, *t*, *s*, *v*, *sh*, *th*, *t*, and *d*.

The data on the audiogram also reveal the type of hearing loss—whether it is conductive, sensorineural, or mixed. This distinction is important since it indicates whether the condition is temporary or permanent and what can be done about it. For example, if the child has poor results on the air-conduction test but good results on the bone-conduction test, his loss is conductive. But if the child has poor results on both air- and bone-conduction tests, his loss is sensorineural.

Compensatory Measures. The audiometric test results may be used to plan compensatory steps for children with hearing impairment. For children with a sensorineural loss, the following steps are essential: (1) Seat children with a sensorineural loss near the front of the room where they can hear verbal explanations and assignments. (2) Talk in a normal voice, but stand reasonably close to them when giving explanations and assignments. (3) Check frequently to see if they understand what is being said. (4) For moderate to severe losses, encourage the child's parents to consider having the child use a hearing aid.

For children with a conductive loss, consider these steps: (1) Encourage the child's parents to take the child to a hearing specialist (called an *otologist*) to evaluate means of correcting the loss through medication or surgery. (2) If the child has frequent colds and earaches, make sure he knows how to blow his nose without forcing mucus through the Eustachian tube into the middle ear. (3) Observe the child closely for times when his hearing is especially bad, particularly after illnesses, and speak more directly to him during those times. (4) Since conductive losses come and go, stay alert for changes in the child's hearing behavior. If it gets worse, notify the parents so they can take the child to the doctor for appropriate treatment.

For children who already use a hearing aid, the following steps are helpful: (1) Again, talk in a normal tone of voice directly to the child. (2) Encourage the child to wear the aid in class and to remove it for active sports to avoid damage or injury to the ear. (3) Explain the function of the hearing aid to the other children to encourage them to accept it as a normal occurrence much like eyeglasses.

For children with a high-frequency loss, pay particular attention to auditory discrimination skills. Do specific diagnosis and instruction for these skills, since these efforts may help children with a high-frequency loss get maximum use from their available hearing. Because such activities are firmly in the teacher's do-

---

figure 3-1

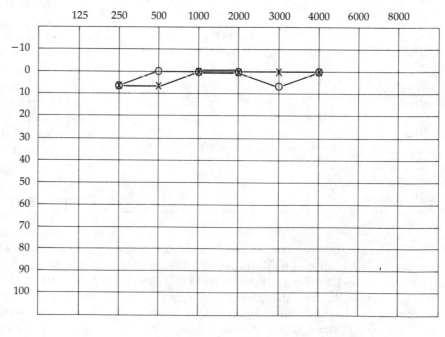

NORMAL-HEARING AUDIOGRAM RESULTS

name _____ age ____ date _____ chart no. _____

address _____ phone _____

city and state _____ birthdate _____

AUDIOMETRIC EVALUATION

Frequencies in Cycles per Second

KEY

Air Conduction

O = Right Ear

X = Left Ear

Bone Conduction

> = Right Ear

< = Left Ear

audiometer _____ tester _____

main, the next section of this chapter concentrates on diagnosis and instruction for auditory discrimination.

AUDITORY DISCRIMINATION

Diagnosis

Auditory discrimination is the ability to identify like and unlike sounds by listening to them. The auditory discriminations most important for success in reading are the abilities used to identify likenesses and differences in letter sounds. These are the auditory discrimination abilities you will need to diagnose and teach.

The more alike letter sounds are, the more likely they are to be confused. The first task in diagnosing these problems is to identify the sounds that are most alike. Begin by considering how you produce letter sounds in your mouth. The *t* sound, for example, is made at the front of the mouth using the tongue against the alveolar ridge (the part of the palate nearest the teeth). It requires breath but no voice. Other sounds like *d* are made in almost the same way, but are voiced. Any sounds like *b* and *t* that share many common features are likely to cause auditory discrimination problems.

__figure 3-2__

HIGH-FREQUENCY LOSS AUDIOGRAM RESULTS

name _____ age _____ date _____ chart no. _____

address _____ phone _____

city and state _____ birthdate _____

AUDIOMETRIC EVALUATION

Frequencies in Cycles per Second

KEY

Air Conduction

O = Right Ear

X = Left Ear

Bone Conduction

> = Right Ear

< = Left Ear

audiometer _____ tester _____

Here is a brief list of sounds that share common features and are likely to be confused:

b-d-t-p

f-v-s-m-n

ch-sh-s-c-k-g

In addition, children with a high-frequency hearing loss often have trouble discriminating among high-frequency speech sounds such as those made by *f, s, sh, wh,* and *h.* These contrasts should also be included in a diagnostic procedure.

Finally, children's abilities to hear likenesses and differences in speech sounds vary according to their position in a word. Thus, the diagnostician must test for discrimination skills at the beginning, middle, and end of words.

Figure 3-3 is a diagnostic inventory of letter sounds suitable for use with children who have hearing impairments or reading problems that may be due to poor auditory discrimination. The test can be administered individually or to a small group. Figure 3-4 is the answer sheet for this test.

Score each child's test and mark the number right on the grid (shown in Figure 3-5) under the appropriate category. Compare the number correct (for each category) with the necessary criterion at the bottom. Circle any score not meeting the criterion. (The criterion for each category has been subjectively chosen. After working with the inventory, you may choose to set it higher or lower.) The results of the diagnostic inventory recorded on the scoring grid are then used to plan instruction.

Active Teaching

Children who have difficulty discriminating between letter sounds can be helped through active teaching. Active teaching is directed toward the specific letter-sound discriminations the child does not make. For example, if the child cannot discriminate between the *b, t, d,* and *p* sounds at the beginning of words, instruction should focus on these specific skills.

Instruction for auditory discrimination follows certain principles. First, children should begin by mak-

─────── figure 3-3 ───────

AN AUDITORY DISCRIMINATION DIAGNOSTIC TEST

Directions: This test is intended to be read aloud. Distribute an answer sheet (see figure 3-4) to each child. Then demonstrate how each item is to be performed. Say:

"Listen to these two words to see if they sound alike at the beginning: *rat-sat.* If they sound alike at the beginning, circle the plus" (demonstrate on the chalkboard). **"If the sound is not alike at the beginning, circle the minus"** (demonstrate on the chalkboard and have the child work the first sample item).

"Now I will say the first words: *mill-hill.*" (Check each child's response.) **"Listen to the next words: *sip-tip.*"** (Check each child's response.)

1. bit-big	6. ten-bet	11. mill-nick	16. sold-some
2. dam-tap	7. five-vine	12. no-nod	17. choose-chop
3. tag-tap	8. fell-fed	13. miss-mind	18. call-cat
4. pun-tub	9. vote-feel	14. chill-ship	19. gum-gut
5. pet-peg	10. safe-fail	15. sob-shot	20. cob-got

"Now listen for the last sound in each word. If the last sound is the same, circle the plus. If the last sound is different, circle the minus."

21. tap-hat	26. let-met	31. room-loom	36. hash-watch
22. fad-mad	27. save-give	32. run-sum	37. back-lag
23. cab-lab	28. groove-roof	33. fan-ran	38. big-pig
24. bib-hid	29. house-fuss	34. hutch-mush	39. tuck-luck
25. cod-pot	30. fluff-muss	35. wish-dish	40. sock-frog

—————— figure 3-4 ——————————————————————————

ANSWER SHEET FOR AUDITORY DISCRIMINATION TEST

Name _____ Date _____

Sample 1 + −

Sample 2 + −

Sample 3 + −

1. + −	11. + −	21. + −	31. + −
2. + −	12. + −	22. + −	32. + −
3. + −	13. + −	23. + −	33. + −
4. + −	14. + −	24. + −	34. + −
5. + −	15. + −	25. + −	35. + −
6. + −	16. + −	26. + −	36. + −
7. + −	17. + −	27. + −	37. + −
8. + −	18. + −	28. + −	38. + −
9. + −	19. + −	29. + −	39. + −
10. + −	20. + −	30. + −	40. + −

ing easy auditory discriminations, then do moderately difficult discriminations, and finally advance to the most difficult discriminations. For example, if a child cannot discriminate between the *t* sound and other similar sounds, begin by asking him to make easy discriminations. Start with contrasts between the *t* and *m*, *r*, and *s* sounds. Read the following word-pairs:

man	**top**	**red**	**top**	**till**
tan	**top**	**ted**	**sop**	**till**

Ask the child whether these words begin with the same or a different sound. If the child responds correctly, present a series of words that begin with sounds that are more alike. Contrast the *t* and *k*, *f*, and *s* sounds in the following word-pairs:

tan	**hip**	**tick**	**sip**	**top**
tan	**tip**	**kick**	**tip**	**top**

If the child can tell whether these words start with the same or different sounds, go on to the most difficult contrasts—those between the *t* and *b*, *d*, and *p* sounds. Read the following word-pairs:

top	**tall**	**time**	**pill**	**tan**
top	**ball**	**dime**	**till**	**tan**

Again, ask the child to tell whether the words begin with the same or a different sound. If he responds correctly, he has learned to make the discriminations you have been teaching. All that remains is to have him practice this new skill for the next several days to ensure its permanence. At the same time, you may teach additional necessary skills based on your diagnosis.

Of course, instruction does not always proceed this smoothly. Sometimes a child will have trouble with some discriminations during the lesson. When

──── figure 3-5 ────────────────────────────

A SCORING GRID FOR AUDITORY DISCRIMATION

INITIAL SOUNDS

Skill	b-t-d-p	v-f-s	m-n	ch-sh-s	c-k-g
Item Numbers	1–6	7–10	11–13	14–17	18–20

names

1. _____

2. _____

3. _____

4. _____

5. _____

| Criterion | 5 | 3 | 3 | 3 | 3 |

FINAL SOUNDS

Skill	t-d-b	f-v-s	m-n	sh-tch	g-ck
Item Numbers	21–26	27–30	31–33	34–36	37–40

names

1. _____

2. _____

3. _____

4. _____

5. _____

| Criterion | 5 | 3 | 3 | 3 | 3 |

this happens, do two things. First, say the words again emphasizing the sound he cannot discriminate. Ask the child to say the words himself, emphasizing the contrasting sounds. Second, call the child's attention to differences in the way each sound is made. For example, the difference between the *t* and *d* sounds is that one is voiced and the other isn't. After the corrective procedure, provide more opportunities for the child to practice on additional word-pairs.

Once you have become comfortable with all of the preceding techniques, you should be able to help many children like Michelle Wilson, whose problem was described in the introduction. You will know whether she should be referred to a hearing specialist, how to interpret the results of a hearing examination, how to diagnose her auditory discrimination problems, and how to teach the skills she needs. This may not ensure her total success in reading, but it will probably help you alleviate some of her problems. You can feel assured that you are doing all the classroom teacher can do.

AN APPLICATION EXERCISE But there is a vast difference between reading all this and actually being able to perform it. To consolidate your skills, do the following application exercise:

1. Identify a child who may have a hearing problem by referring to the list of symptoms of hearing impairment.

2. Review the child's school records for information about possible hearing difficulties in the past.

3. Have the child's hearing tested with an audiometer. (Usually, the school nurse can do this.)

4. Interpret the results according to the information in this chapter.

5. Administer the auditory discrimination test (Figure 3-3) included in this chapter.

6. Teach the child to discriminate between any letter sounds that confuse him by using the techniques described in this chapter.

DECODING: MONOSYLLABIC WORDS

will enable you to

1. Diagnose children's general and specific needs for instruction in decoding monosyllabic words

2. Teach children to decode monosyllabic words using one of three methods—letter-sound, analogy-and-contrast, or sight-word

David McCann detests school. He spent one year in kindergarten, two more in first grade, and another year in second grade. He is now in third grade although it is actually his fifth year in school. The other children know he is older than they and that he "flunked." They sometimes make fun of him, especially during reading. He is a member of the low reading group but still can't do the work expected of him. When the teacher writes *tan, can, van, bin* and *tin* on the board, David can't read the words. Neither can he read his "baby-level" reader nor any of the library books on the free-reading table.

David's cumulative folder says that he is of "low socioeconomic background," which means that he doesn't have good winter shoes or a warm coat, that he gets a free lunch, and that he usually doesn't have the necessary dime, quarter, or half-dollar for special class projects. His cumulative folder also says that he is absent a lot. His I.Q. score, now three years old, is 96.

At the last parent-teacher conference, the teacher told Mrs. McCann that David would have to learn to behave. The teacher reported that he had been teasing the girls. (He had darted into the girl's lavatory, actually.) She also said that he was disruptive when returning from the playground. (He had once run across the desk tops in the classroom.) And he used inappropriate language in school. (He occasionally said "Shit!" when he struck out in soccer-baseball.)

David is in a self-contained classroom along with twenty-seven other children. Several other children have similar problems, but David's are the most extreme. His test scores indicate that he should stay in the regular classroom rather than go to a special class. David will be eligible for help from the remedial reading teacher for two, forty-minute sessions a week, but not until the second semester. Before reading further, analyze the problem and make recommendations.

What is the nature of the problem? _____

_____

_____

What are the classroom teacher's responsibilities to David? _____

_____

_____

_____

What are the classroom teacher's responsibilities to the other children? _____

_____

_____

_____

Very specifically, what should the classroom teacher do first? _____

_____

_____

David has one clear problem: he cannot "decode." He cannot even sound out phonetically consistent words. For example, when asked to read a list of phonetically consistent words:

mad	ban	tap
had	ben	tad
sad	bin	tab
pad	bun	tag

David makes the following errors:

"Mix" for "mad"
"Hop" for "had"
"Pin" for "pad"

"Ben" for "ban"
"Bet" for "ben"
"Buy" for "bin"

"Time" for "tap"
"Told" for "tad"
"Two" for "tag"

If David cannot sound out words with such obvious sound-spelling relationships, he will probably have even more trouble with words that have more difficult sound-spelling relationships. To help David, the teacher must understand what decoding is and the mental operations involved, why it is important for reading, how to diagnose a child's decoding ability, and how to teach specific decoding skills to a child who needs instruction.

DECODING

Decoding is the process of translating print into speech. This process can be broken down into several steps. Let us imagine that the child encounters a printed word that he has never read before—*mop*. The decoding operation is as follows:

1. Visual Discrimination: The reader must perceive the distinctive shape and unique order of the letters. He must recognize that the black-and-white squiggles before him (*mop*) are different from other combinations of black-and-white squiggles he has seen before (such as *top, cop,* or *sop*).

2. Letter Sounds: The reader must then associate the three letters in *mop* with their most frequently occurring sounds.

"M-m-m-m-m-m" *and* "ŏ-ŏ-ŏ-ŏ-ŏ" *and* "p (uh)"

3. Sound Blending: The reader must blend these three separate sounds into a single utterance. In the process, he must deal with a considerable amount of distortion that occurs when one sounds out a word. Actually, he must blend the three sounds into a reasonable approximation of the actual word and then intuit what the word is in normal speech.

"M-m-ŏ-ŏ-p . . . M-ŏ-ŏ-p . . . Mop!"

4. Speed. To read well, the reader must do this decoding operation very rapidly—almost at the subconscious level.

5. Fluency and Inflection. Finally, he must supply what the printed word cannot—expression. The reader must imagine how each word and phrase should be uttered—whether it should be loud or soft, clipped or slurred, joyful or doleful. Inflection, this final, imaginative step, is important in decoding if reading is to be meaningful and enjoyable. In a sense, the reader must "decode" the author's intent even as he unlocks each word.

The child must know how to decode in order to learn to read. If he can be taught to decode—to translate from print to speech—rapidly, accurately, and imaginatively, his reading ability will approach his oral language ability. He will be able to read and will probably understand anything within his command of the language.

Understanding the decoding process is tremendously important in helping children like David. He is eight years old and has an average I.Q. Logically, David should have a speaking vocabulary numbering in the thousands of words. But David's reading vocabulary is fewer than fifty words. If David can be taught to decode, his reading vocabulary will probably increase to the size of his speaking vocabulary. With children like David, diagnosis and instruction for decoding ability must come first.

DIAGNOSING DECODING SKILLS

The purpose of diagnosis is to save time and effort. There are hundreds of decoding skills and subskills. You will want to know which ones individual children have and have not mastered. Precise diagnostic information will help you plan lessons for children at their exact point of need. Later, using the original diagnostic information as base-line data, you will be able to determine which skills children have mastered as a result of instruction.

A good diagnostic procedure for decoding skills should do several things. First, it should tell you who needs instruction for specific skills. Second, it should require an absolutely minimal amount of time to administer. Third, it should provide a means of assessing skills attainment after instruction. That is, it should help the teacher discover whether the child is achieving mastery of skills as instruction proceeds.

The Pairs Test

Here is one plan for diagnosis. Begin by administering an informal reading inventory (as described in Chapter 1). The child's IRI performance will indicate whether he has problems with decoding. If the child can read through the selection at the third-grade level with relative fluency, it is reasonable to assume that he has mastered virtually all monosyllabic decoding skills. But if the child reads haltingly at the lower levels or if he has numerous substitution errors, you should assume that he needs further diagnosis and instruction in decoding.

If the child's instructional reading level is at the third-grade level or below, the next step is to administer the Pairs Test of Decoding Skills. The Pairs Test consists of 114 "minimal-discrimination" word-pairs. Each word-pair is used to test the child's ability to decode a specific element. For example, the first word-pair *(rat-bat)* is intended to test the child's ability to decode initial consonant *b*. The first subtest from the Pairs Test is shown in Figure 4-1.

Administration procedures are similar to those for the informal reading inventory. The child has one copy to read from and you have a copy to mark on. You pronounce the first word in each pair and ask the child to pronounce the second word. If the child pronounces the second word correctly, mark your copy accordingly. If the child gives an incorrect response, record his error on your copy.

To interpret the results, it is necessary to know how each item works. Consider the word-pair *rat-bat*, an item designed to test decoding of initial *b*. When you say the first word, you supply much of what the child needs to decode the second word. If the child has the necessary decoding skills, he will notice that the critical difference between the two words is the first letter. He may then produce the correct sound for *b*, blend the sound with those already supplied, and read the word correctly. In this event, you may conclude that he knows how to decode words with initial consonant *b*. If he does not say the second word correctly, however, you may logically conclude that he needs instruction on decoding words with initial consonant *b*.

After administering the test, you record on the record-keeping grid the number of errors the child made for each subset of items (see Figure 4-2). There are two items in each subset. If the child makes any errors in a subset, you may assume that he needs some instruction for that skill. At this point, you must decide just how to conduct the necessary instruction.

---
figure 4-1

SUBTEST A: INITIAL CONSONANTS

1. toy-boy	12. sip-hip	23. hip-rip
2. fin-bin	13. lump-jump	24. cut-rut
3. tap-cap	14. tab-jab	25. cap-sap
4. sup-cup	15. dot-lot	26. mix-six
5. hot-dot	16. tap-lap	27. bell-tell
6. him-dim	17. rap-map	28. hip-tip
7. sun-fun	18. hill-mill	29. fin-win
8. sell-fell	19. nub-nib	30. tell-well
9. tap-gap	20. get-net	31. nip-yip
10. sob-gob	21. kin-pin	32. jell-yell
11. cut-hut	22. bat-pat	

—— figure 4-2 ——————————————————————————

SUBTEST A   INITIAL CONSONANTS

name	b	c	d	f	g	h	j	l	m	n	p	r	s	t	w	y
1. _____																
2. _____																
3. _____																
4. _____																
5. _____																
6. _____																
7. _____																
8. _____																
9. _____																
10. _____																
11. _____																
12. _____																

TEACHING DECODING SKILLS

To teach a child to decode, you should have in your command several alternate teaching strategies. Three useful strategies presented in this section are the *letter-sound technique*, the *analogy-and-contrast technique*, and the *sight-word technique*.

The Letter-Sound Technique

The letter-sound technique is effective in teaching a child to decode words that have logical and consistent sound-spelling patterns. For example, the sound-spelling relationship of words like *tin, sack, hill, hop,* and *pat* can be considered logical and consistent because the consonants are pronounced in predictable ways and the vowels are all short. The letters strongly imply just how the words sound. In contrast, words that have illogical sound-spelling patterns are such words as *was* (pronounced "wuz"), *the* (pronounced "thuh"), and *come* (pronounced "kum").

There are several specific steps in using the letter-sound technique:

1. Identify the skill to be taught through diagnosis.

2. Write a list of phonetically consistent words containing the skill to be taught.

3. Teach the child each prerequisite skill for decoding the words on the list. The prerequisite skills are: visual discrimination, letter sounds, and sound blending.

4. Provide opportunities for the child to practice the skill.

The Pairs Test of Decoding Skills is a useful instrument for identifying the skill to be taught. If the skill to be taught is decoding words with initial consonant *d*, list at least ten phonetically consistent words beginning with *d*.

dot	dull	dim
dip	den	dog
dock	dig	dug

To provide contrast, list some similar words that begin with different letters. For example, use *got* to contrast with *dot*. This list is used to guide instruction during each of the following steps. Do not attempt instruction without an adequate list.

Next, teach each prerequisite skill for decoding the phonetically consistent words. The prerequisite skills are visual discrimination, letter sounds, and sound blending.

"D" Words	Contrasting Words
dot	got, hot, pot
dip	lip, sip, rip
dock	rock, sock, lock
dent	bent, lent, sent
den	hen, pen, men
dig	big, pig, rig
did	bid, kid, hid
dim	him, rim, slim
dog	log, bog, fog
dug	rug, tug, jug
dab	cab, lab, tab

Visual Discrimination. This is the ability to distinguish one thing from another by looking at it. To decode, the child must be able to tell one letter from another, even if the letters are very similar or if they are written in an unfamiliar style. The child must know the critical differences between such letters as *b* and *d*, *m* and *w*, *g* and *p*, and many others.

If the child has difficulty telling letters apart, his skill can be increased through active teaching. This may be accomplished by asking the child to make discriminations of increasing difficulty. For example, at the easiest level of discriminations, the teacher may ask the child to distinguish between very dissimilar letters at the beginnings of words. To do this, the teacher writes the following words on tag-board charts and asks the child to tell whether the first letter of each pair is alike or different.

EASIEST DISCRIMINATION LEVEL

<u>d</u>ot	<u>d</u>im	<u>r</u>ig	<u>d</u>og	<u>m</u>en
<u>r</u>ot	<u>s</u>it	<u>d</u>en	<u>d</u>id	<u>d</u>en

If the child can make this easy discrimination, the teacher presents another chart requiring closer discriminations and asks the child to tell whether each word-pair begins with the same letter.

MODERATE DISCRIMINATION LEVEL

<u>d</u>ig	<u>d</u>ull	<u>k</u>in	<u>t</u>in	<u>d</u>ock
<u>h</u>ot	<u>d</u>id	<u>d</u>im	<u>d</u>on't	<u>d</u>ip

If the child can make this more difficult discrimination, the teacher presents a third chart requiring the most difficult letter discriminations and asks the child to tell whether each word-pair begins with the same letter.

HARDEST DISCRIMINATION LEVEL

| <u>d</u>ip | <u>b</u>id | <u>d</u>ill | <u>d</u>im | pot |
| <u>d</u>og | <u>d</u>id | gift | <u>d</u>ot | <u>d</u>ent |

If the child can discriminate between these beginning letters, the teacher may assume that he can visually discriminate well enough to decode. Once the child shows that he can discriminate, he is ready to learn the sounds of the letters.

If the child has difficulty at any of the three discrimination levels, however, do several things to help him. Write the two single letters that confuse him on a chalkboard and ask him to use one finger to trace the shapes of the two letters on the board. Then ask him to describe the difference between the two letters. His response for a *b-d* discrimination might be something like, "This one has a round part on this side [motioning], but the other one sticks out on the other side."

Letter Sounds. To teach letter sounds for decoding, the teacher must know what sound to give each letter. Begin by thinking of the consonants and vowels separately. The consonants may be further classified into two groups: continuants and stops. *Continuants* are sounds that can be held, like "m-m-m-m-m." *Stops* are sounds that cannot be held, like the *t* sound. The consonant continuants are: *f, h, l, m, n, r, s, v, y, z.* The consonant stop sounds are: *b, c, d, g, j, k, p, q, t,* and *w.* There is little question about what sound to give the continuants, since each represents a separable entity in speech. But stops do not represent easily separable entities. They are always followed by a vowel sound when they are pronounced. For example, the sound for *d* is usually followed by one of the vowel sounds as in *dig, do,* or *dim.* It is important in teaching letter sounds to minimize the vowel sounds that normally occur after each stop sound. So the sound for letter *d* should be taught as a very brief sound. It should not be "d-u-u-h-h-h," it should be "d—(uh)," with an absolute minimum of emphasis on the inevitable "uh" sound. Other stop sounds should be treated similarly.

Vowel sounds are a much more difficult problem than consonant sounds since each vowel is given a different fundamental sound and is also shaded in sound by the preceding and following consonant. It may be best to simplify the problem when teaching by presenting only the short-vowel sounds at the outset.

Consonant	Recommended Sound	Sound to be Avoided
b	"b" (soft vowel)	"b-u-u-h-h"
c	"k" (no vowel)	"k-u-u-h-h"
g	"g(uh)" (soft vowel)	"g-u-u-h-h"
j	"j(uh)" (no vowel)	"j-u-u-h-h"
k	"k" (no vowel)	"k-u-u-h-h"
p	"P" (no vowel)	"p-u-u-h-h"
q	"qu" (soft vowel)	"q-u-u-a-a-h"
t	"t" (no vowel)	"t-u-u-h-h"
w	"wu" (soft vowel)	"w-u-u-h-h"

After the child has learned to decode words with short vowels, he can then learn the long-vowel sounds and how to identify words that contain them.

Teach the letter sounds as a memorization task. Write the letter for the sound to be taught on the chalkboard. Tell the child what sound to say when he sees the letter. Do not confuse the child with unnecessary explanation. Simply say, "This is *d.*"

Have the child say the sound whenever you point to the letter. Since this is a stop sound and cannot be held, instead of pointing to the letter in a way that implies that it should be held, just tap it. Write a few letters on the board that the child has already mastered and ask him to give the sounds as you point. Avoid introducing more than one letter sound at a time. Use other letters that are unfamiliar to the child, whose sounds he does not know, for contrast. Teach the sound for only one new letter at a time.

After the child can give the sound of the letter, he is ready to begin sound blending.

Sound Blending. This prerequisite for decoding may be considered as a series of minute operations. For example, if the child is to decode the word *rim,* he must perform each of the following operations:

1. Visually discriminate the first letter—*r.*

2. Associate the appropriate sound with the letter— "r-r-r."

3. Hold the sound and look at the next letter.

4. Visually discriminate the second letter—*i.*

5. Associate the appropriate sound with the letter— "i-i-i."

6. Hold the sound and look at the last letter.

7. Visually discriminate the last letter—*m*.

8. Associate the appropriate sound with the letter—"m-m-m."

9. Say the final sound to conclude pronunciation of the word.

10. Overcome the distortion involved in sound blending to identify and pronounce the undistorted word.

The new aspect of sound blending lies in steps three, six, and nine: holding the sound and looking at the next letter. Overcoming distortion, the final step, is also new.

To teach sound blending, write two letters the child has learned on the chalkboard. Draw a dot and a directional arrow underneath the two letters. Tell the child, "Say the sounds as I point." Then point to the letters from left to right. Write several combinations involving the new letter and previously learned letters. Repeat the process, "Say the sounds as I point." After the child has mastered this process, do the same thing with three-letter combinations: "Say the sounds as I point." Encourage the child to hold each sound until he is ready to produce the next sound. He should say "s-s-a-a-m-m-m-m" instead of "s-s (pause) a-a (pause) m-m." This results in less distortion while decoding and makes the final step—overcoming distortion—easier.

When the child has mastered the previous step, ask him to undistort the word he has sounded. Say, "What's the word?" The child should then give the word using normal pronunciation, "Sam!" He is now decoding.

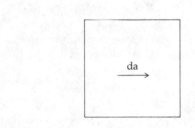

The Analogy-and-Contrast Technique

The analogy-and-contrast technique is a system of teaching the similarities and differences among word groupings. It is useful for teaching the child to decode many more words than the letter-sound technique. Whereas the letter-sound technique is useful for teaching only those words that have *highly consistent* sound-spelling relationships, the analogy-and-contrast technique can be used with two categories of words—those that have highly consistent sound-spelling relationships and those that have less consistent sound-spelling relationships. For example, words that follow the consonant-vowel-consonant (cvc) pattern have highly consistent sound-spelling relationships. These include such words as *pin, tin, kin, sin,* and *din.* Words containing *r,* diphthongs such as *oi,* and variant vowels such as *aw* have less consistent sound-spelling relationships, as shown in the list below.

Words with "R"		Words with Diphthongs	Words with Variant Vowels
four	fair	join	eat
sore	bear	house	pain
corn	their	plow	boat
roar	parent	boy	food
war	care		crook

Although the analogy-and-contrast technique has the advantage of being useful with many more words than the letter-sound technique, it has the disadvantage of requiring that the child intuit much more than the letter-sound technique requires—sound-blending and some letter-sound relationships for example.

The analogy-and-contrast technique may be considered in specific steps. The teacher must:

1. Identify the skill to be taught through diagnosis.

2. Write a list of words with analogous and contrasting sound-spelling relationships.

3. Have the child memorize the first word on the list.

4. Teach the subsequent words by analogy and contrast.

5. Provide opportunities for the child to practice the skill.

Use the diagnostic procedures described in the first part of this chapter to identify the skill to be taught. The analogy-and-contrast technique is often used to teach several decoding skill objectives during the same lesson. Thus, the teacher may select several elements, such as initial letter sounds *m, r, s, f,* and *t* for instruction. The instructional process is described below.

Analogy Word List. Begin by writing a list of phonetically similar words that contain the decoding elements selected for instruction. Show the child the list to illustrate how each element is used. For example, if the objectives for instruction are initial sounds *m, r, s, f,* and *t,* you will need a few words beginning with each.

m	r	s	f	t
man	ran	sit	fun	top
mud	rip	sun	fat	tap
mop	roll	sag	fin	tug
mix	run	sad	fell	tin
mill	rug	sup	fix	tan

Contrasting Word List. This list should illustrate the significant contrasts between words. It must contain pairs of words differing by only one element—the element to be taught. For *m* you would need:

man	mix	sop	mill	top	sill
fan	fix	mop	fill	mop	mill

For *r:*

run	fat	rug	red	rip	roll
fun	rat	mug	fed	lip	toll

For *s:*

sit	run	sag	sad	mix	sip
fit	sun	rag	mad	six	rip

For *f:*

fun	rat	fin	fell	fix	fill
run	sat	tin	tell	six	mill

For *t:*

top	tap	tug	tin	tan	rip
mop	sap	rug	sin	man	tip

Teach the first word by memory. For example, if you wish to teach the child to decode words beginning with the letter *m,* begin by teaching a single word like *man* by memory. To do this, print the word *man.* Show the printed word to the child and say, "This word is man." Then have the child practice the word. Say, "What is this word?" and then have the child respond. After the child has had several opportunities to practice the response, go on to the next step.

Teach subsequent words by analogy and contrast. Begin with analogy. Write the word list for *m* on the chalkboard:

<u>m</u>an

<u>m</u>ud

<u>m</u>op

<u>m</u>ix

<u>m</u>ill

Pronounce the first word for the child, emphasizing the initial sound, "This is M-m-m-an!" Ask the child to read the other words, "If this is *man* (point), the next word must be _____?" If the child has difficulty, supply the missing sounds for him. That is, if he says, "It's m-m-m . . . ," supply the missing parts of the word as a prompt.

Next, teach by contrast. Write one or several word-pairs from the contrasting list on the board. Have the child practice decoding by telling him the name of the first word and asking him to say the second word. For example, write *pan* and *man* on the board. Say, "If this word is *ran,* the next word must be _____." Continue this procedure through several word-pairs, prompting the child when necessary.

Provide opportunities for the child to practice. Write a series of phrases using the pattern words. Have the child practice by reading them aloud. For instance, write and practice:

_____ is a man.	_____ and a mill.
_____ in the mud.	_____ on the mud.
_____ is a mop.	_____ in the mix.

Next write the pattern words in simple sentences and have the child practice reading them.

Mop up the mud.

Mix the mud.

The mug is tan.

Repeat the process for any group of words with similar sound-spelling relationships. Keep the teacher-child interaction lively and fast paced. Remember that your goal is to teach the child to decode words that he has never seen before fluently and accurately.

The Sight-Word Technique

The sight-word technique is useful for teaching the child to recognize words that fall into two categories: first, words that have inconsistent sound-spelling relationships such as *was* (pronounced "wuz"), *the* (pronounced "thuh"), or *come* (pronounced "kum"); second, words that are difficult for the reading level of the child but are necessary to sustain the story line. For example, *astronaut* would be a very difficult word at the first-grade reading level but is used to make the story more interesting.

Sight-word teaching has both assets and liabilities. While it is an extremely simple teaching technique that can be used with little advance preparation, one drawback is that sight-words may be learned very quickly during a skill session and forgotten very quickly after the lesson is over. Second, sight-words are often confused with other words that have similar shapes. For example, the following words would be easily confused if they were learned only by the sight-word method:

come   cone   cane   cain

Another liability is that learning a word by sight does little to help a child decode words he has never seen before. For example, if a child learns the word *man* as a sight word, he may not be able to decode other words as a result of his new skill. But if he learns *man* by means of letter-sounds or analogy, he has a powerful tool for decoding words he has never read before.

There are three specific steps in using the sight-word technique. The teacher must:

1. Identify words that should be taught as sight-words.

2. Write the words on cards for presentation.

3. Teach the child to recognize the word at sight by:
   a. telling the child the word.
   b. having him practice the response.

To identify the words to be taught as sight-words, examine the actual story you want the child to be able to read. Identify all words that fit either of the following descriptions.

1. The word has a highly inconsistent sound-spelling relationship. That is, it is not pronounced in the way its spelling would logically suggest.

2. The word is quite long or difficult for the level.

After you have selected the words to be taught, write the words on index cards, printing the letters in clear, unadorned script. You may wish to draw or attach an appropriate picture to the back of the card to be used as an aid to memorization.

Teach the child to recognize the word at sight. First, have him look at the card and say, "John, this word is *astronaut*." Then have him practice the response. Say, "What is this word?" He should have an opportunity to say the word many times in response to its printed form.

Present the child with at least five sight-words during the practice session. This will provide him with some generalized contrasts. Without something to use as a contrast, the child would have no reason to know why *any* word wouldn't be *astronaut*.

AN APPLICATION EXERCISE

Up to now, you have been reading about methods of teaching decoding. To operationalize these skills, perform the following application exercise.

1. Select a story written at the first- or second-grade reading level.

2. Select a passage from the story that is less than one hundred words long.

3. Identify the words in the passage that are appropriate for teaching by each of the following methods: letter-sound technique, analogy-and-contrast technique, and sight-word technique.

4. Prepare materials suitable for teaching the words using all three techniques.

5. Practice the teaching techniques with an adult partner.

6. Review this chapter to determine whether you have mastered each technique.

7. When you feel you have mastered each method, administer the Pairs Test to a child to diagnose his skills and use your teaching techniques to help him learn to decode.

Once you have performed these exercises, you will have attained above-average skill in teaching decoding. This special competence is a great advantage to you as a teacher when you encounter children like David, whose case was described at the beginning of this chapter. Although you will not be able to solve such children's environmental problems—inadequate income, medical care, and diet—you will be able to help such children in significant ways. Being able to diagnose their reading problems and teach at the point of need is a large part of what is within your power as a teacher. You may know that helping children like David learn to read will also help alleviate their emotional and social problems.

DECODING: MULTISYLLABIC WORDS

will enable you to

1. Diagnose children's general and specific needs for instruction in decoding multisyllabic words

2. Teach children to decode multisyllabic words by using appropriate teaching procedures

After children have learned to decode most monosyllabic words, they are ready to learn to decode multisyllabic words. Teaching multisyllabic decoding requires that you as the teacher have some additional information and a different set of diagnostic and teaching skills from those described in Chapter 4 on decoding monosyllabic words. Specifically, you need to understand the mental operations involved in multisyllabic decoding; you need to know how to write, administer, and interpret a diagnostic inventory; and you need to master techniques of actively teaching children to decode multisyllabic words. This chapter is designed to help you acquire these skills.

Multisyllabic decoding is the act of translating multisyllabic words such as *astronaut, motorcycle, synthesizer,* and *lepidoptera* from print into speech. Doing this requires the following complex mental operations. First, the word is visually segmented. For example, the word *astronaut* is visually segmented into three parts *as-tro-naut.* Next, monosyllabic decoding methods are applied to each segment to sound out an approximation of the actual word. Finally, to overcome the distortion, the reader searches his memory for a word that is similar to the slightly distorted word he has just said. If it is a word he knows, he will overcome the distortion and pronounce it—"astronaut." The mature reader repeatedly applies this sequence of mental operations at great speed as he reads. But children who are learning to read must be taught precisely how to do it.

DIAGNOSING SKILL IN MULTISYLLABIC DECODING

This is a two-part plan for diagnosis. The first part consists of inspecting the results of the informal reading inventory—a general indicator of the child's need for instruction. The second part consists of administering a diagnostic inventory—a precise indicator of the child's need for specific kinds of skill instruction. Each procedure will be described in detail.

Begin diagnosis by reviewing the results from an informal reading inventory. The first indicator of the child's need for instruction in multisyllabic decoding is his instructional reading level. Generally, children reading between the second- and fourth-grade instructional levels frequently need instruction, since these are the reading levels where multisyllabic word attack is usually emphasized and learned. If the child reads at a lower level, it is probably best to emphasize monosyllabic decoding skills—a prerequisite to success in multisyllabic decoding. If the child reads fluently at a higher level (fifth- or sixth-reader level), he has

probably already mastered multisyllabic decoding.

Review the teacher's scoring sheet from the IRI, which indicates the child's specific oral reading errors between the second- and fourth-reader levels. Note whether the child has made many errors in decoding multisyllabic words. Note especially whether he makes frequent, definite errors on multisyllabic words. If he makes errors such as substitutions on multisyllabic words, you may logically infer that he does need further diagnosis and instruction for multisyllabic decoding.

Analyzing the child's reading behavior on the IRI more closely will identify the specific types of words he has missed. Are the words compounds or contractions? Are they words with affixes or words that have nonmeaningful separate syllables? Such analysis is temporarily useful for planning instruction, but a more detailed analysis of the child's skill will be even more beneficial.

To make a detailed analysis, first list the more difficult multisyllabic words that occur in the reading materials you plan for the child to use. Second, identify each of the words in the list as a compound, root word with affix, or other multisyllabic word. The following definitions further clarify each classification:

Compound: A word formed from two separable words such as *rowboat, airplane,* and *everyone.*

Root with Affix: A separable word with a letter combination added that modifies the meaning.

Multisyllable: A word that may be divided into syllables for reading, but the separate syllables generally do not have independent meanings.

Third, write a series of diagnostic subtests that require the child to segment visually each multisyllabic word. To make interpretation easier, group similar words together on the inventory. For example, group words with the same affix or words with similar vowel structure. Figure 5-1 shows a model diagnostic inventory.

The information grid can be used for setting up flexible "skill groups." That is, from analyzing the data on the record-keeping grid, you may choose to call together just the children who need help on a particular skill, teach the precise skills they need, and then disband the group. You would repeat the process for instruction on other skills. In addition, you may use the diagnostic information to individualize assignments. Basal-reader workbooks often devote twenty or thirty pages to multisyllabic decoding, implying that every child should do every page. You may use the diagnostic information to select the specific pages each child needs to do.

You may use the information to control group interaction. Consider a situation when you must call an eight-member group together despite the fact that only three of the children need instruction for a particular skill. If normal group interaction is uncontrolled, the five children who have prior mastery of the skill will probably dominate the interaction. On the other hand, if you know who really needs help and who does not, you will be able to direct your teaching toward those children who need instruction.

TEACHING MULTISYLLABIC DECODING

The diagnostic procedures described above will help you identify children's reading skill needs and plan for instruction. The next step is active teaching. Regardless of the multisyllabic pattern involved, the essential teaching pattern is the same. The child must be taught to segment multisyllabic words visually in logical places, to decode each syllable, and to blend the

—— figure 5-1 ——

A MULTISYLLABIC DECODING TEST

PART ONE: COMPOUNDS

Directions: Draw a line to show how each of the following words should be divided for reading. For example; rowboat is row/boat.

1. microwave	6. supertool
2. championship	7. teammate
3. repairman	8. bowstring
4. typewriter	9. nickname
5. horseshoe	10. shipshape

Criterion: 9/10

PART TWO: MULTISYLLABLES

Directions: Draw a line to show how each of the following words should be divided for reading. For example, apple is divided as follows: ap/ple.

1. company	1. dragon	1. doodle
2. expensive	2. favor	2. battle
3. message	3. pupils	3. eagle
4. furnace	4. amaze	4. single
5. collect	5. camera	5. metal
6. mystery	6. neither	6. gravel
7. permission	7. season	7. approval
8. shelter	8. proper	8. example

Criterion: 7/8 for each set

PART THREE: ROOTS AND AFFIXES

Directions: Identify and write the <u>root</u> word. For example, for <u>going</u>, the root word is <u>go</u>.

1. solving _____
2. demanding _____
3. eyeing _____
4. fiercely _____
5. highly _____
6. tightly _____
7. thoughtfully _____
8. successfully _____
9. hopefully _____
10. disinterest _____
11. disengage _____
12. admiration _____
13. vibration _____
14. resurrection _____

1. worthless _____
2. hopeless _____
3. painless _____
4. tastiest _____
5. fastest _____
6. strangest _____
7. tangled _____
8. practiced _____
9. awakened _____
10. astonishment _____
11. judgment _____
12. stillness _____
13. darkness _____
14. forgiveness _____

Criterion: 3/3 for each subset

___

syllables into an approximation of the word. If the word is familiar, the child will probably overcome the distortion and produce the actual word.

The basic pattern for teaching multisyllabic decoding has five steps:

1.   (Planning) Write a list of words similar to the ones the child could not segment on the diagnostic test.

2.   (Teaching) Present one word on the chalkboard and show how it is divided.

3.   (Teaching) Ask the child to sound out the separate parts of the word.

4.   (Teaching) Ask the child to say both parts of the word together and to say the actual word.

5.   (Teaching) Provide opportunities for the child to apply the new skill with similar words.

Step One.   Write a list of words similar to those the child had trouble with. For example, if diagnosis indicates that the child cannot segment words with the

vowel-consonant/consonant-vowel (vc/cv) pattern, the following list of words would be appropriate for teaching:

1. stubborn
2. patter
3. rabbit
4. stagger
5. picture
6. fasten
7. halter
8. panda
9. tanner
10. certain
11. after
12. window
13. circus
14. picnic
15. system

Step Two.   Present one word on the board and show how it can be divided. For example, the word *stubborn* could be presented as follows:

(Write)   stubborn

(Say)   "Words like this one must be divided in order to sound them out. I would divide this word between the two consonants."

(Write)   stub/born
        vc/cv

Step Three. Ask the child to sound out the separate parts:

(Say) "Sound out the first part." (Point)
"Now sound out the second part." (Point)

Step Four. Ask the child to undistort the word:

(Say) "Say both parts together."

"Now tell me what the word is."

Step Five. Provide opportunities for the child to apply his new skill. Repeat the process with subsequent words. Ask the child to divide them, sound out the parts, and overcome the distortion.

Other words that contain roots and affixes are presented in the same way. For example, the word *boldly* could be presented as follows:

(Write) boldly

---
figure 5-2

A SCORING GRID FOR SYLLABICATION

	Compounds	Multisyllables*			Roots and Affixes	
		vc/cv	v/cv	/cle	ing	ly
names	9/10	7/8	7/8	7/8	3/3	3/3
1.____						
2.____						
3.____						
4.____						
5.____						

Roots and Affixes (cont.)

	fully	less	est	ed	dis	tion	ment	ness
names	3/3	3/3	3/3	3/3	3/3	3/3	3/3	3/3
1.____								
2.____								
3.____								
4.____								
5.____								

SCORING KEY

O=Meets criterion. No instruction needed.

/ =Does not meet criterion. Instruction is needed.

X=Has attained the criterion after instruction.

*The letter markings stand for the consonant-vowel structure of multisyllabic words.

vc/cv	v/cv	/cle
shel/ter	dra/gon	sin/gle

(Say)   "Words like this one must be divided in order to sound them out. I would divide this word by separating its root from its ending."

(Write)   bold/ly

The remaining steps are the same as for any other multisyllabic word. Ask the child to sound out the separate parts, to undistort the word, and to practice on similar words like *coldly*, *badly*, and *likely*.

If the child has difficulty, you may choose to prompt him by pointing out significant features such as vowel and consonant structure. But be careful in doing so. Many generalizations for decoding are confusing to children, since the principles are more complex than the task they are supposed to clarify. Also, many generalizations are misleading because of the number of exceptions that occur in reality. For these reasons, it is probably best to do what was done in the teaching example. Give a clear model. Avoid confus-ing explanations. And emphasize the commonalities between words with a similar structure.

AN APPLICATION EXERCISE   Up to now, you have been reading about teaching multisyllabic decoding. To operationalize this skill, do the following application exercise.

1.   Select reading materials at the second-, third-, or fourth-grade reading level.

2.   Make a list of the multisyllabic words in the materials and use them to write a diagnostic inventory.

3.   Administer the inventory to a child whose instructional reading level matches the materials.

4.   Teach the child the multisyllabic decoding skills he needs to read the materials.

MOTIVATION

will enable you to

1. Organize the classroom reading program into three essential components

2. Use reinforcement techniques to maximize attainment of skills

3. Minimize unnecessary paper-and-pencil assignments

4. Provide for students' personal interests, individual reading levels, and individual attention spans

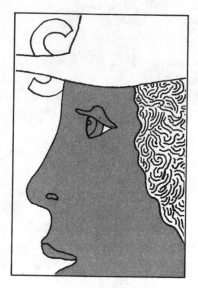

During reading, Files Shipman shows all the initiative of bread dough without yeast. He gazes blankly at the page during silent reading and offers no comments during the discussion that follows. In the library, he wanders from shelf to shelf, unable to choose a book he likes. He seldom turns in written assignments without being prodded. And when he does, they are usually unreadable. Files's mother says that he hates reading.

But Files comes to life for other activities. He is an aggressive contender in any ball game. He has an old car body in his backyard which he tinkers with for hours at a time. And Files has earned his bear badge (with two arrows) in cub scouts. In art, his creativity and imaginative flair result in bold, eye-catching works.

This discrepancy in behavior puzzles his teacher. How would you analyze the problem? _____

_____

_____

What would you do about it as a teacher? _____

_____

_____

_____

_____

At the very least, Files has a motivational problem. If Files could articulate its various aspects, he would tell us that the stories in the basal reader that he is expected to read in class are too hard. When he reads aloud, the other children look knowingly at one another. Then later, on the playground or in the hall, they taunt him for being "dumb." When Files attempts to read the stories to himself, there are just too many "hard words" for the story to mean much. As for the subsequent paper-and-pencil assignments, they're impossible. Not only do they require understanding the story, but they also require composition, penmanship, and spelling skills he doesn't have. Past experience has shown Files there is little difference between the teacher's displeasure over his usual work and her displeasure over no work at all. Files knows he can't please her and is convinced that she doesn't like him.

To motivate children like Files who have soured on reading does not require that you have mystical powers or a charismatic personality. Instead, it requires that you understand how children get turned off to reading and that you know how to turn them back on. In other words, you must know how to organize the reading program in ways that are inherently motivating to children. You must also learn how to conduct yourself in ways that enhance children's self-concepts and reading achievement.

The techniques of this chapter will help you become a "motivation specialist." Motivational techniques will be described in relation to the most important components of any reading program.

THE COMPONENTS OF MOTIVATION

Motivation may be increased by organizing the reading program into three components. During the first, or *teacher instruction component*, the teacher actively instructs children. Such teaching activities as presenting concepts at the chalkboard, introducing assignments, and holding discussions are familiar aspects of the teacher instruction component. The second is an *independent application component.* This is usually a follow-up activity designed to reinforce the concepts presented by the teacher. Reading assigned stories, answering comprehension questions, and doing workbook exercises are common activities in the application component. Third is a *self-selection component.* At this point, children are allowed to make choices according to their individual needs and interests. Children may read library books and magazines, play reading games, and do special projects involving reading science or social studies, for example. Each motivational component requires careful consideration of its intended purpose and the techniques necessary to achieve it.

MOTIVATION DURING THE TEACHER INSTRUCTION COMPONENT

Most teacher instruction in reading occurs in small groups or on a one-to-one basis. Motivation can be increased through the use of planned reinforcement. Consider the model of the teaching process:

figure 6-1 —————————————

SCHEMATIC DIAGRAM OF THE INSTRUCTIONAL PROCESS

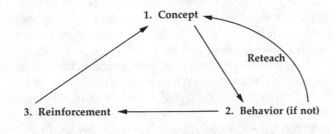

The model describes a simple teaching pattern to be used during any instructional process. As you teach even a brief lesson, learn to move through the steps rapidly.

The steps of the instructional process may be described as follows. Before you teach, decide precisely what you think the child should be able to do as a result of your instruction—that is, the *concept.* The concept or skill to be taught is selected through diagnosis. The skillful teacher has learned to identify the child who needs instruction and can specify what the child should be able to do once he has mastered the skill.

Teach the concept. Rely on modeling or demonstrations for teaching rather than long-winded explanation. Learn the techniques (presented in earlier chapters) of breaking complex skills into their component parts. Remember that you, the living and breathing person, can present concepts and make them come alive far more effectively than any form of printed material.

Ask the child to demonstrate his understanding and mastery by applying the skill being taught. This is step two of the sequence—*behavior.* If your teaching has been effective and the child performs the skill successfully, go on to the next step.

Reinforce appropriate responses. You will need to use many methods of reinforcement: positive statements and gestures, written systems for positive feedback, and body language. (These methods will be discussed further.)

If the child has not learned the correct response, do not reinforce him. Simply say "No" and *reteach* the skill by going back to the first step in the sequence. This time, break it down into simpler parts, use simpler language, or use a completely different teaching method.

REINFORCEMENT

Reinforcement may be considered in four basic categories, starting with the highest form: (1) intrinsic, (2) social, (3) token, and (4) nutrient. Each method may be defined as follows.

Intrinsic Reinforcement. This is the highest form of reinforcement. It is internal and may be described as the innate satisfaction of having done something that is personally meaningful.

Social Reinforcement. This level of reinforcement comes from other people. Approval, praise, friendship, and status are common forms.

Token Reinforcement. This level of reinforcement occurs when one receives an object that represents social approval.

Nutrient Reinforcement. This form of reinforcement is simply food. In the classroom, small amounts of food are sometimes given to children to reinforce desired behavior.

Each form of reinforcement has both advantages and disadvantages for classroom use. In addition, some forms are associated with "moral" implications. You will ultimately need to consider these factors for yourself and make a personal judgment based on what you believe.

Intrinsic Reinforcement

Intrinsic reinforcement has the highest status in educational literature. John Dewey was the foremost proponent of intrinsic motivation. He believed that if the child were involved in highly educative experiences related to his present life's needs, there would be no need for other "artificial" reinforcers.

To maximize intrinsic motivation, you must identify the child's present interests and concerns. For instance, for Files Shipman, the most pleasurable reading materials would be related to his current projects. Since he is in cub scouts, the teacher could assume that he would probably be interested in books about camping, building things, outdoor adventure, or science projects—all related to cub scouting. Or, if Files had just been given a puppy, the most logical selections for intrinsic motivation would concern care of dogs, training dogs, and building doghouses. He would probably respond enthusiastically to such materials and find them innately satisfying. Clearly, this is education at its best.

However, there are inherent difficulties associated with relying exclusively on intrinsic motivation. First, it is almost impossible to maintain a constant supply of individualized materials and experiences that will appeal to the needs and interests of every child in the classroom. Second, the teacher is powerless if the child does not respond in the predicted manner. Third, a child's interests and concerns, especially a young child's, are capricious. By the time you secure materials to fill an expressed interest, the child may shift his attention to something else. If a child fails to respond to your efforts to capitalize on his interests, social reinforcement may be an effective alternative.

Social Reinforcement

Social reinforcement is the workhorse of the classroom. Social reinforcement may be verbal or nonverbal and it may come from the teacher or from other children. You can increase classroom motivation by learning to use both modes.

Verbal praise is especially important. Children with reading problems become terribly discouraged about school and develop negative, destructive self-concepts. The appropriate use of verbal praise can help such children learn to read and thus improve their self-concepts. You must learn to vary your praise, to use it at appropriate times, and to mean it when you use it, since children can almost always detect false praise.

Learning to give varied forms of praise requires conscious effort and habit development. Unfortu-

nately, most people are not in the habit of giving praise even when it is richly deserved. Cultural habit restricts the occasions when adults praise one another and, even more sharply, restricts their capacity to accept praise. To help motivate children, you need to develop a repertoire of reinforcing statements. Pretend for a moment that one of your students has just shown that he has learned to do something he couldn't do before. Attempt to list ten different forms of verbal praise that you could use. Now memorize the list so that you are able to vary your praise automatically instead of relying on a single, shopworn phrase.

Praise children for desirable behavior—both reading behavior and classroom behavior. This may be a difficult task because children who may need praise the most often seem to deserve it the least. You must learn to watch closely those children who are most in need of praise. Learn to catch them in the act of mastering a reading skill, selecting a library book they can read, practicing good study habits, or of being friendly to others, and consistently reinforce them with verbal praise.

Habits of using verbal praise are catching. If you praise often, students tend to emulate your behavior. They will begin to notice, value, and comment on others' accomplishments. By learning to reinforce, you are generating a positive, supportive attitude among all of the children in your classroom.

Can praise be overdone? Can children receive too much praise? Conceivably, yes. But it is unlikely to happen when you must distribute your praise among thirty children. Thus, in the classroom, giving too much praise is virtually impossible.

Nonverbal reinforcement is also important. Conscious nonverbal reinforcement such as smiles, nods, handshakes, hugs, and pats-on-the-back may be used to reinforce desired behavior, especially with young children. In addition, you should try to become aware of your unconscious nonverbal behavior. You must recognize that you transmit a constant stream of nonverbal messages to your students through your body posture, tone of voice, facial expressions, and proximity. Although studies of the mechanics of this communication process are still in their infancy, research has shown that teachers unconsciously transmit their academic expectations to their students, and this transmission significantly affects the children's ultimate achievement in school. This evidence would indicate that the value judgments you make about your students will affect your teaching behavior. It would follow that negative value judgments could have seriously damaging consequences.

Examine your own attitudes about individual children for negative bias. Ask yourself if you have acquired negative attitudes about a particular child's habits of cleanliness, his morals, his parents' behavior, his religion, or his place of residence. Examine your thinking about his ethnic background. Do you have stereotypes concerning people of this ethnic group? Do you regard the child as much like yourself or as very different? Guard especially against making value judgments about children on the basis of comments in their cumulative record folders. Make sure that you are not unconsciously looking for reasons to expect reading failure—for causes that will explain why little should be expected from the child academically.

Make a practice of seeing the positive aspects in children's backgrounds. For example, if the child comes to school dirty, it may be because he must get ready for school by himself. In this event, consider his self-reliance instead of his dirty neck and ears. If the child swears, it may be that such behavior gains acceptance from his peers. In such a case, avoid making strong moral judgments and taking harsh punitive measures; simply advise him that such language is unacceptable in school.

Look for positive ways to interpret the information in children's cumulative records. If the file says there are "no books in the home," interpret this to mean you should have extra books for him in the classroom. If the folder says that he "comes to school hungry," investigate the federal free-breakfast and lunch programs in your school. In any event, be positive about the child's ability to learn since expectations of success or failure are almost certainly telegraphed to the child through your nonverbal behavior.

Token Reinforcement

Children who do not respond to social reinforcement will often respond to token reinforcement, since it is more tangible and longer lasting. Tokens commonly used in classrooms are stars, plastic markers, theater tickets, and certificates of various kinds. These tokens—linked with verbal praise—are given to the child as a reward for desirable behavior. In other words, when using token reinforcement, tell the child what he did to deserve the token—that is, what it signifies. Say something like, "I'm giving you this plastic chip because you learned to use 'M-m-m-m-m.'" Remember that the token has little value in itself. It is the visible symbol of an accomplishment—that the child worked hard, learned something important, or behaved appropriately. Your attitude and comments establish the token's value.

Token reinforcement is a "mixed bag." It has some constructive uses as an alternative or supplement to social reinforcement. But it creates more problems than the higher forms of reinforcement. For instance, token reinforcement is constructive when it

encourages a child to be more interested in his own progress and gratified by it. But it can be destructive when it encourages a child to compete with other children. For this reason, a chart that shows an individual's daily progress or the skills attained is among the best token reinforcers. In contrast, a chart that shows group progress, or who gets the most stars, is among the worst.

Nutrient Reinforcement

Nutrient reinforcers are small bits of food, usually raisins, M&M candies, or sugar-coated breakfast cereals, presented to children when they exhibit the behavior the teacher has tried to elicit. This method is used with very young children who do not respond to the higher levels of reinforcement. It is usually paired with one of the higher levels of reinforcements, such as praise, until the child learns to respond to praise alone. Then the nutrient reinforcer is phased out.

In summary, the teacher must select those kinds of reinforcement that appear most effective. In general, intrinsic reinforcement and social reinforcement are the most useful forms in the classroom. Token reinforcement should be used if social reinforcement alone is ineffective. Nutrient reinforcement should be used if none of the other forms works. This recommendation is *not* based on the notion that lower forms of reinforcement are improper; the higher forms of reinforcement are simply more convenient and practical for teaching.

Let us consider for a moment the value judgments other teachers sometimes make on the morality of various levels of reinforcement. Social, token, and nutrient reinforcers are often lumped together and called "bribes." This is interesting when one considers that adults depend on reinforcers in numerous ways. Social reinforcement occurs when others compliment us or give us approval through friendliness and acceptance. Good bosses and supervisors are expected to notice and remark on adequate job performance and to reward superior performance with a raise in salary or a "Christmas bonus." Token reinforcers take the forms of bowling trophies, war medals, diplomas, and certificates. Nutrient reinforcers appear as hospitality and gifts.

Willard Waller, in *The Sociology of Teaching*, calls the schools "museums of virtue."[1] He contends that the schools maintain puritanical moral codes far removed from those of society at large. The notion that

---

[1] Willard Waller, *The Sociology of Teaching* (New York: Russell & Russell, 1932).

only intrinsic motivation is really "moral" is a prime example. He suggests that if we as teachers really regard intrinsic motivation as the only moral alternative, we should refuse our paychecks, turn in our college diplomas, and carefully negate any rewards in social status for being teachers. If we believe that *only* intrinsic motivation is moral for children, perhaps we should live by the same code ourselves.

MOTIVATION DURING THE INDEPENDENT APPLICATION COMPONENT

During the application component of the reading program, children are usually assigned to do independent reading and seatwork. The purpose of these activities is to have students learn to apply each new reading concept. Ideally, the application component will follow the active teaching component and will be directly related.

It is common to find classroom motivation at a low ebb during the independent application period for several reasons. Often, children are asked to do far too much busywork. The assignments are sometimes unrelated to the skills they are learning; others are boring or too difficult. In addition, the application period may be too long. It is possible to avoid most of these pitfalls by following a few pointed suggestions.

First, keep the independent application component short—no more than twenty to twenty-five minutes. The easiest way to do this is to organize a self-selection component to provide follow-up activity for an additional fifteen to twenty minutes, thereby reducing the need for a lengthy application period.

Second, base the independent application component on diagnosed need. This usually requires reorganizing instructional materials. Instead of using workbooks and having children do each page in order, build a "skill file." A skill file is made by obtaining a set of file folders, marking each one with the name of a separate reading skill, and filling each folder with exercises and other materials related to that skill. The file is then used to facilitate making independent application assignments. For example, if children are receiving instruction for initial consonant *d* during the active teaching session, from the appropriate skill file you will be able to assign them a worksheet for the same skill—quickly and conveniently. This scheme reduces the total number of worksheets the children need to do and eliminates unnecessary exercises.

Third, make sure that children are working at their appropriate reading level. This can sometimes be difficult because children and parents often pressure

the teacher into assigning a reader that is too difficult for the child to read. The child may struggle along reasonably well during the teacher instruction sessions, but when asked to read or to do seatwork independently, the constant struggle with the material makes him *very* susceptible to distraction and discouragement. To avoid this problem, be certain that each child is placed at his independent reading level for independent work.

Finally, continue to praise children for appropriate behavior. Although you may be very busy instructing other children during this time, you may elect simply to stop instructing others occasionally to notice and praise children who are working productively. Or, if you could bring an aide into the classroom to help you during the independent application period, you could ask that he or she observe the children and praise them for appropriate behavior, just as you would.

MOTIVATION DURING THE SELF-SELECTION COMPONENT

The self-selection component is a time when the child is permitted to choose his own reading activity. Its fundamental purpose is for the child to develop the lifelong habit of reading. Its secondary purposes are to encourage personal initiative in skills attainment and to promote the use of many types of books. The self-selection component occurs every day for fifteen to twenty minutes. During this time, children are on their own. They learn to select and perform various activities independently, leaving the teacher free to instruct others.

The self-selection component is a necessity rather than a luxury. For children who are slower than their classmates, this is one of the few times when they are not under pressure. It is a time when they can seek out materials at their own reading and interest levels and read them on their personal time schedule. For children who have the constant frustration of being "behind," this is often a unique experience. The self-selection component is also a necessity for you. It is a worthwhile activity that frees you to work with others and, once underway, it requires minimal planning time. It does not add to the ever-higher mountain of papers to correct.

To ensure a successful self-selection component, you should begin by organizing a classroom reading center and obtaining materials for it. You must also teach the children how to use the self-selection period well. The next section of the chapter suggests how to accomplish this.

Organizing a Classroom Reading Center

The classroom reading center is an area used to display all kinds of reading materials. It is also a place where children can go to read. Think of it as a handy mini-library designed to increase motivation.

The organization of the classroom reading center has much to do with its effect on motivation and warrants careful planning. Visual appeal, for example, is important. Restaurants and clothing stores do more business if they are attractive, and so do reading centers. Make your reading center visually distinct from the rest of the room by decorating it in bright, contrasting colors. Boundary markers such as hanging glass beads also help to make the center visually distinct. The reading center should also provide a change of location and seating—an important motivator for children who spend much of the school day riveted to their desks. Thick carpeting or bean-bag chairs make excellent seating, since they project informality and offer a different body position from a rigid school chair. Ironically, the center may also be motivating for some children if it allows them to escape from distractions, especially friends, in order to read undisturbed. To achieve this effect, locate the reading center out of the direct line of vision for the rest of the class. Also, consider whether two or three study carrels might be useful for students seeking seclusion.

The reading center requires furniture and other facilities. Ideally, some desirable items would include: (1) display shelves for books and magazines, (2) a bulletin board, (3) an electrical outlet, (4) comfortable seating, (5) study carrel dividers, and (6) a tape recorder with earphone headsets. After you have organized the center, you are ready to select appropriate materials.

Selecting Materials. There are many types of materials you should consider for your reading center. These include books, magazines, newspapers, filmstrips, and recorded materials. Each will be discussed in turn.

Library (trade) books are most important. To increase motivation, determine your students' areas of interest and select books accordingly. Interests can be determined by circulating a questionnaire, by interviewing, or simply by observing children. Whichever method you choose, you will want to know about books they have enjoyed previously, projects they are engaged in, trips they have taken or plan to take, problems they are having, and television programs they like. Each will provide clues to books that may be personally meaningful. Once you have gathered this information, you can select library books children will enjoy.

Trade books must also be chosen by reading level, since children with reading problems may tend to select overly difficult books to avoid the embarrassment of being seen with "babyish" books. Unfortunately, many books at their interest-maturity level may be too difficult for them to read. To reawaken the interest of poor readers, it is often necessary to seek out high-interest, low-vocabulary books. It is also necessary to reassure these children that reading books that present no difficulty is quite all right.

Magazines are excellent for use in the reading center. To increase your supply, ask the school librarian for back issues of such magazines as *Boy's Life, Jack and Jill, Popular Mechanics, Wee Wisdom, Playmate, American Girl, Horse Lovers, School Bulletin, Ranger Rick, Children's Digest, Seventeen,* and *National Geographic.* Children will probably be motivated to do more magazine reading if magazines are used for recreational reading rather than for report writing. For students who won't read anything else, you may also get some "forbidden" materials such as comic books or the comics sections from Sunday newspapers. There are some children who will *read a Bugs Bunny, Batman,* or *Archie* comic book, who won't read anything else.

Tape-recorded stories and books are highly recommended for use in the reading center. Children who are poor readers are usually poor listeners as well, but their skills can be increased through practice. You may wish to tape-record trade books so that children may listen and read at the same time. This practice increases reading skill, probably by demonstrating how print can be interpreted fluently and imaginatively. Solicit the help of some extroverted friends to read stories into the tape recorder. For best results, ask them to read at a moderate pace and to overdramatize. The more dramatic the reading, the better the children will like it.

There are countless potentially suitable materials for your reading center. Consider the advantages of using materials such as:

1. Stories written by other children and bound into short books.

2. Filmstrips to be read on small, individual viewers.

3. A stimulus for reading, such as a live rabbit and several books about rabbits.

4. Reading games to be played by two or more students.

5. Basal readers and other schoolbooks from previous years.

6. Stationery, mailing envelopes, stamps, and a classroom mailbox.

7. Rate-building devices for individual use.

Although classroom reading centers take many different forms—depending on location, furniture, materials, and decoration—the essentials are always the same. Centers are intended to motivate children to read by providing for individual interests, reading rates, and proficiency levels. Reading centers are also intended to help you teach by keeping some children productively engaged while you instruct others. These results can be achieved only if children know how to use the centers.

Teaching Children to Use the Classroom Reading Center. Children must learn to do four things: select books, operate equipment, keep records, and behave appropriately. One simple way for a child to select a book at an appropriate level is to have him read a single page and then subject it to the following test: (1) "Hold up a finger for each word you don't know. If you hold up three fingers, the book is probably too difficult." (2) "After reading the first page, close the book and ask yourself if you know what it was about. If you don't know, the book is probably too difficult." Remember that children need to be supported and reinforced when they do this, because the child with the most serious reading problems may be subjected to ridicule for selecting a book at his reading level.

Children must know how to operate any equipment in the center, such as tape recorders, filmstrip viewers, and reading pacers. They must also know how to play any games that are available. You might appoint a few children as special assistants to help those at the reading center in order to minimize interruptions as you instruct other groups.

Children should learn to keep a simple, anecdotal record of their activities in the center. This record will help you evaluate their reading preferences and progress. Provide each child with an activities logbook with space for four daily entries. Figure 6-2 is a sample entry showing the desired information. Teach the children to make appropriate entries as a language arts lesson. Then use their logbooks to advise them, to select additional materials, and as an occasion to praise their efforts.

Finally, children must learn to behave appropriately during the self-selection period. Children are so accustomed to receiving directives in school that they need to be taught how to operate when given unusual freedom. To initiate children into the self-selection process, begin by offering a simple choice between two or three activities. Make sure they have all the information necessary to carry on the activities. As time goes on, gradually expand the number of choices.

Reinforce children who are using the reading center well. Praise children for selecting appropriate books, for keeping records, for maintaining the center in good order, and for being courteous to others.

Hold a discussion on reading center activities at frequent intervals. Have various children describe what they did. Talk about how the self-selection period could be made better. Help the children understand that personal freedom is dependent on appropriate behavior.

figure 6-2 ——————————————

SAMPLE LOGBOOK ENTRY FOR READING CENTER ACTIVITIES

LOGBOOK ENTRY

time in: _____ time out: _____

activity: _____

comment or request: _____

_____

AN APPLICATION EXERCISE Up to now, you have been reading about motivation. You have learned that motivation can be increased by consistently using reinforcement techniques, examining one's own attitudes about children, providing children with materials at a suitable reading level, and by structuring the reading period into three different components—active instruction, application, and self-selection. To consolidate these skills, do at least one of the following applications.

MOTIVATION IN THE ACTIVE TEACHING COMPONENT

1. Find a child to work with. Diagnose his reading skill needs using the techniques presented in earlier chapters of this book.

2. Determine the kind of behavior you wish the child to achieve. Plan to teach him this behavior through a sequence of small steps.

3. List the reinforcers you plan to use as he exhibits the behavior you are teaching.

4. Teach the skill and use the reinforcement techniques you have planned.

MOTIVATION IN THE INDEPENDENT APPLICATION COMPONENT

1. Obtain a set of materials commonly used for independent application assignments (workbooks, ditto masters, games, other activities).

2. Identify the most important objective of each separate page, worksheet, or exercise and divide the materials accordingly.

3. Construct a skills file with a separate file folder for each objective.

4. When you teach, use the skills file to individualize (and to minimize) paper-and-pencil assignments.

MOTIVATION IN THE SELF-SELECTION COMPONENT

1. Organize a classroom reading center within a regular elementary school classroom.

2. Select materials for the reading center by gathering and using information about children's reading levels and interests.

3. Teach a small group of children to use the center without close supervision.

When you have done these things, you will have achieved a special competence in motivational techniques. This special competence will help you teach children like Files Shipman. If he is discouraged and convinced that he cannot learn, your mastery of reinforcement techniques will go far toward changing his attitude. If he seems to have a short attention span, providing materials aimed at his personal interests, his reading level, and supplying a variety of activities will almost certainly make a difference. And if he has mistaken his previous teachers' frustrations for personal dislike, your own satisfaction with an effective approach to motivation may project a different image and lessen his alienation.

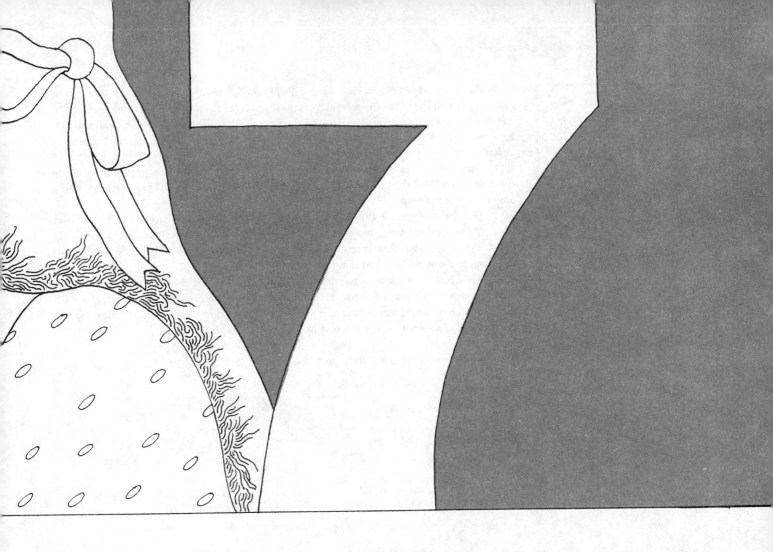

BASIC COMPREHENSION: THE DIRECTED READING LESSON

will enable you to

1. Improve the child's ability to concentrate on what he is reading

2. Improve the child's ability to read for facts, organization, and main ideas

3. Increase the child's reading vocabulary

4. Enable the child to understand the meaning of literary devices

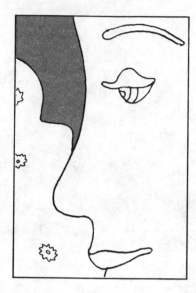

Sally Barclay's reading behavior is most perplexing. She seems to be very interested in reading. When she visits the school library, she selects a wide range of books related to her interests in horses, crafts, pioneers, and recently (like other sixth-grade girls), romance. She shows the books to her approving teacher and parents and then, conspicuously, she makes a great show of reading.

But her interest is short-lived. After the first few pages—a chapter at most—she loses interest. And the cycle repeats itself: another book, approval from others, and a short fling at reading.

IRI results indicate that Sally's oral reading is quite good up to seventh-reader level. After oral reading, her responses to comprehension questions are reasonably good. When reading silently, Sally seems to be reading very fast. But following silent reading, her comprehension is terrible.

This behavior puzzles her teacher. Sally's interest in books contrasts sharply with her practice of reading little. Her comprehension after oral reading contrasts with her comprehension after silent reading. And her interest in pictures, particularly in the crafts books, outweighs her interest in the printed explanations.

How would you analyze Sally's problem? _____

_____

_____

_____

What would you do about it? _____

_____

_____

_____

_____

_____

READING COMPREHENSION

Sally clearly has major problems with silent-reading comprehension and minor problems (if any) with decoding. Therefore, an analysis of her problem must be related to how reading comprehension occurs. Reading comprehension begins with decoding. To comprehend, the reader must decode with considerable fluency. At the same time, he must supply many elements of oral language that are missing in print. For example, the reader must imagine how words and sentences would be spoken. Which words are stressed? Where do pauses occur? How loud are these words and sentences? And what is the right intonation? Reading is, by nature, an imaginative act. To make print meaningful, the reader is imagining at the

subconscious level during silent reading. These operations must all be done at the rate of about 140 words per minute—approaching that of normal speech—so as not to lose the train of thought.

Reading comprehension also requires concentration. The reader must mentally shut out distractions to concentrate on the task at hand. Concentration must be sustained until the meaning is extracted—a task that may extend over several pages or a chapter of more difficult materials.

Reading comprehension is based on oral language development. The reader must know what each word means—knowledge that comes mainly from listening and speaking. The sentence patterns must be familiar. In English, word order is an important aspect of sentence meaning. If the child uses a sentence pattern in speech, comprehending the same sentence pattern in print is easy. But if the sentence pattern is unusual or unfamiliar, comprehension is obstructed. The reader must understand unusual ways in which language is used. Figurative speech, for example, aids or impedes comprehension depending on the child's language sophistication. Some highly verbal children would derive meaning from the phrase "I had butterflies in my stomach," while other children would wonder how the butterflies got there.

Reading comprehension is related to experience. In abstract subjects especially, first-hand experience is the decisive factor between understanding a concept while reading and being mystified. Think how well you would comprehend a book about plumbing, for example, if you have never fixed a pipe. Or consider your possible comprehension of a sailing manual if you have never sailed a boat. Comprehension of some topics, particularly those involving motion and spatial relationships, seems to require direct, first-hand experience.

Reading comprehension is inseparable from thinking and should not be viewed as a mechanical process different from other intellectual activity. After a reader decodes print, he must process and interact with the message. This calls for mental processes similar to other nonreading intellectual acts. If a child decodes well but does not understand the message, he may have a "thinking" problem.

Reading comprehension is emotionally related. The child's self-image as a reader affects his comprehension. If the child knows from previous classroom experience that he is capable of understanding, his prospects for further improvement are enhanced. If he has been taught from previous experience that he cannot comprehend what he reads, his negative self-image may make him less teachable.

Finally, these various factors are interrelated. Homer Barnett, a cultural anthropologist who studies human dynamics, has formulated a law of human behavior: "One damn thing leads to another." His "law" fits reading comprehension precisely. For this reason, instruction in reading comprehension is more global than instruction in decoding. This chapter presents a method for teaching children to comprehend by focusing on various factors within a single lesson.

THE DIRECTED READING LESSON

The directed reading lesson is a widely used method for teaching reading to small groups. It is also the method recommended in most basal readers. Although there are variations in the format of the directed reading lesson from one basal series to another, the similarities are greater than the differences. Once you become familiar with teaching directed reading lessons, you will be able to teach reading comprehension effectively regardless of the basal reader you use.

The directed reading lesson consists of two parts usually presented on two successive days. The first part is the story introduction, which lasts from five to ten minutes. The children then read the story independently. The second part is a directed rereading of the story, which lasts from fifteen to twenty minutes on the following day. The section below describes the objectives and procedures for each part of the directed reading lesson.

Planning

A successful directed reading lesson requires planning. The first step is to identify children who need similar instruction and group them together. Generally, children who read at the same instructional reading level may be grouped together for instruction. (The informal reading inventory, described in Chapter 1, is used to determine children's functional reading levels.) For effective instruction, limit the group to ten children or fewer.

The second step is to obtain materials. Basal readers appropriate to the child's reading level are recommended. Such readers are useful because each story is of similar difficulty and their teaching guides offer useful suggestions for teaching a directed reading lesson related to each story. Other materials, such as library books that have short, episodic chapters, are also appropriate. Often trade books (also called library books, or simply, children's books) have more exciting stories than basal readers. In addition, simple trade books may be more socially acceptable to intermediate-grade children than primary-level readers that may evoke ridicule from classmates. Finally, there are many high-interest, low-vocabulary books written especially for older children who read poorly. These books are generally available from reading clinicians and special-education teachers. Any of these materials may be used for teaching directed reading lessons. The most important criteria are that they be at the children's instructional reading level and that they contain material the children enjoy.

The third step in planning the directed reading lesson is to find something constructive for the rest of the class to do while you work with a small group of children. If you teach reading to three groups at three different levels (as discussed in Chapter 1), you may schedule the other children to do application assignments and self-selected activities while you meet with each separate group. For example, if you have sixty minutes each day for reading, your schedule for a single day might look like this:

Time	Group 1	Group 2	Group 3
11:00	Meet with the teacher.	Application assignment.	Self-selection period.
11:20	Application assignment.	Self-selection period.	Meet with the teacher.
11:40	Self-selection period.	Meet with the teacher.	Application assignment.
12:00	End of the reading period. Lunch time.		

This schedule is most typical of the intermediate grades. The primary grades usually schedule more time for reading—often ninety minutes a day. In this event, you could use the one-hour schedule (shown above) in the morning and then use a half-hour period in the afternoon for flexible skill grouping on decoding skills.

The First Session

This part of the directed reading lesson has four steps.

Step One: Teach the child the vocabulary he must know to understand the story.

Step Two: Relate the story to the child's past experience.

Step Three: Establish a purpose for reading.

Step Four: Provide time for the child to read the story and accomplish the set purpose.

Each step is directed toward an important aspect of reading comprehension that can be translated into specific objectives. And each step must be accomplished in a very few minutes. Since time is precious, you must know precisely what to do for each step.

Vocabulary is a prime factor in comprehension; thus, the first step is to teach word meanings necessary to understand the story. Your objective is to teach the children to use each new word in an original sentence and to give examples of how the word can be used. To accomplish this objective, identify the most difficult words in the story before meeting with the group. Then teach the words by the three methods described in Chapter 8—language-interaction, word-elements, or context—until the children have attained the objective. To avoid the distraction of unfamiliar words, do most of the vocabulary teaching before the children even open their books.

Meaningful reading is also a product of past experience. But children may not have had a relevant past experience to associate with a given selection. Your task, then, is to provide a vicarious experience similar to the one they have missed. If they have never visited a farm, for example, you may take them on a vicarious visit to the farm using pictures from magazines. (A large picture file is a great asset in teaching comprehension.) Your objective would be for the children to describe the various creatures and activities on the farm, just as they might do if you could take them on an actual field trip.

Often, children may have had a real-life experience related to the reading selection, but they do not recognize the relationship. Your task in this case is to probe into their past experience to point out relationships to the story. For example, if the selection is about spiders, ask the children to describe their previous experiences with, and beliefs about, spiders. Then suggest ways in which the story they will read is related to their own past experiences. The ultimate objective of this activity is for children to learn to identify and describe independently, the relationships between stories and their own life experiences.

Reading comprehension requires concentration. But many children with comprehension problems are easily distracted. Your task is to help them attain a stronger mental set or sense of purpose for reading. To do this, review the selection to determine why it might be worth reading from a child's point of view. Again, using the example of the story about spiders, the teacher might say: "Today we'll read about spiders. As you read, find out all the ways spiders are helpful to man so that we can talk about it later." The children would then read with this set purpose in mind. Or, with a mystery story, the enjoyment comes from anticipating and predicting what will happen or who did the deed. Biographies may often be read for the sense of being in on the lives of great people. Books on science may be read to understand natural or technological events we sometimes take for granted. On a lower order, there are some things we read simply because we must, like forms and directions. Whatever it is, identifying a purpose for reading the story will help you teach comprehension.

Once you have established the purpose for reading with the children, your objective is for them to keep this purpose in mind as they read and to demonstrate that they have achieved it when they have finished reading. The demonstration may be either verbal or written. You may simply tell the children what the purpose is, have them read the story silently, and then hold a follow-up discussion to find out whether they have achieved it. Or, you may devise a written assignment related to the purpose of the selection and then evaluate their attainment of the objective by analyzing what they have written. In any case, children can be helped by practice in reading for a purpose.

After you have taught unfamiliar vocabulary, related the story to the children's past experience, and established a purpose for reading, let the children read the story. Allot a generous amount of time in relation to the length and difficulty of the selection and tell the group how long they will be given. Then leave them alone to read the story as you work with another group.

The Second Session

The second part of the directed reading lesson consists of three steps.

Step One: Evaluate and reinforce the objectives achieved during the first session.

Step Two: Have the children reread the story silently, in parts. As you do this, identify children's specific difficulties with comprehension and teach as the need becomes evident.

Step Three: Along with the children, plan some enrichment activities that logically follow from the content of the story.

Again, each step is directed toward an important aspect of reading comprehension and can be translated into specific objectives.

Reading comprehension, like other forms of academic achievement, is affected by the child's feelings and beliefs about himself. Therefore, another important step in instruction for comprehension is to encourage children to achieve and to reinforce them when they progress. The second session, then, begins with an evaluation of progress accompanied by much praise and encouragement.

Begin by evaluating children's attainment of the stated purposes of reading the selection presented in the first session. If the children were given a written assignment related to the selection, review their work with them and praise them for the things they have done well. Note that this is the opposite procedure of the traditional school practice of identifying and punishing (with red pencil marks and low grades) for mistakes children have made. If the purpose of reading

the selection was discussed aloud, praise the children for accomplishing the objective.

Most often, the purpose of the first reading is to attain the larger ideas and events in a reading selection. Therefore, you should elicit evidence of the children's understanding of these concepts and events and reinforce them with verbal and nonverbal reinforcement for attaining this knowledge from reading. If a child has not attained the desired knowledge from reading, withhold your praise. But do encourage him. Say, "This is sometimes a very hard thing to do. But we are going to reread the story now to understand it better." Then go on to the next step, directed rereading.

The directed rereading activity is related to several aspects of comprehension. Reading comprehension requires imagination. The reader must imagine how words and sentences are spoken, especially when reading dialogue. He must form a mental picture of a setting from a written description. Sometimes, the reader must envision a series of actions. If a child does not do this, he may be helped through particular kinds of instruction. For example, you may have noticed during oral reading that some children do not read with expression. They clearly are not imagining how words and sentences would be spoken if the characters were real people. Your instructions in this case might be for them to reread a short section silently and to imagine how it would sound if the characters were present. Then have each child read a passage aloud and reinforce those who read dialogue in imaginative and expressive ways.

In the same way, if the story requires the reader to visualize a scene or object from a written description, ask the children to draw the scene or object from the author's description. Then reinforce children for including details mentioned in the selection and for adding other details that are consistent with the author's intent.

Reading comprehension is a product of the similarity between the reader's language and the language in print. For example, the word order of a sentence may create a problem. A child may understand the sentence, "Bobby struck his friend with his fist," but not understand, "His friend Bobby struck with his fist." The child understands the first form because it is one he uses and is confused by the second because he does not use it. Consequently, another objective for the rereading period is for children to translate unusual sentence patterns into familiar patterns as an aid to comprehension. To accomplish this, identify sentences that have an unusual word order. Call these to the children's attention and have them translate the form to one they commonly use.

Figurative language may cause similar difficulties. Some children are very literal in their understanding of speech. If the text reads, "The city was a desert, and Joe's Bar the only oasis," they envision the city as a sandy place and Joe's bar as having palm trees. The logical objective for children who do not understand figurative language is to translate the figurative phrase into one they understand. After instruction, children will be able to give the literal equivalent for any example of figurative speech used in the story. This, incidentally, is quite different from labeling figurative speech. There is no need for the child to say, "This is a simile" or "This is a metaphor"; all he needs to do is change whatever it is into a literal form.

The rereading session is ideal for doing additional work on extending periods of concentration. A child may have difficulty sustaining his interest long enough to read a whole story with comprehension. Therefore, another objective of the rereading session is to increase the child's attention span from its present length to the length of a whole story. To accomplish this, divide the story into segments. At first, choose very short segments of one to three paragraphs and ask a question or two about the most significant events in each segment before the children reread. Then have the children reread the story in segments silently to find the answer to the question. Then reinforce those children who can answer the question after reading the segment.

Obviously, all this is too much to be included in a single session. It was never meant to be. To attain these objectives, approach them one or two at a time. For example, you may decide that the greatest problem with a group of children is lack of expressiveness. If so, use the rereading time just for developing expressiveness. Or, you may find it more workable to have two objectives, such as increasing concentration and translating figurative language, and you may work on both during a single lesson. The main point is to establish definite objectives in keeping with the nature of comprehension and then to work systematically toward attaining those objectives during the directed rereading lesson.

The last step of the second session is planning enrichment activities. These activities are related to two other aspects of reading comprehension. First, reading comprehension is inseparable from thinking in general. Second, all aspects of reading comprehension, especially reading and thinking, are interdependent. Therefore, things we read about in books enrich thought—a fact we take for granted. Various thought-provoking activities also aid reading comprehension—something we may seldom consider.

Thus, there are many things that don't look very much like reading you can have children do to facilitate comprehension. For example, comprehension of a reading selection about spiders may be enhanced through enrichment activities involving live spiders. There are several possible reasons for this. First, experience and involvement are related to interests. If the children are encouraged to capture a spider, build a cage for it, and keep it alive, they are very likely to be much more interested in reading about spiders. Second, closely observing spiders provides a clearer mental image that facilitates understanding verbal description. Third, watching spiders in action calls up various reflections and hypotheses. Perhaps the child thinks, "I wonder what it's like to be a spider," or "I wonder how it makes that web." This form of independent inquiry is the stuff from which the child sets his own purpose for reading.

All this implies that it is worthwhile to encourage children to plan projects related to their reading. These projects strengthen the interrelationship of reading comprehension and thinking. In addition, they communicate a powerful message to the child about the uses of reading. Taking part in enrichment activities demonstrates, even to the child with a comprehension problem, what reading is about. Enrichment projects are planned during the second session of a directed reading lesson and carried out during the self-selection component of the reading program.

This format for a directed reading lesson is intended for use with children like Sally (whom we described in the introduction), who may read fluently but do not comprehend. The emphasis is on the essential skills in reading comprehension—concentration, vocabulary, reading for specific information (mainly facts), figurative language, sentence patterns, oral interpretation, and reading for a purpose (usually for summarization). This particular format is best suited for children whose instructional level is between low third- and high fourth-reader level. For children at a lower level, the format should include a greater emphasis on decoding. For children at a higher reading level, the plan should include greater emphasis on the higher-level comprehension skills of analysis, synthesis, and evaluation. The application exercise that follows is intended for use with a child at the third- or fourth-reader level.

AN APPLICATION EXERCISE

Up to now, you have been reading about the directed reading lesson. But there is a vast difference between reading about anything and learning to do it. To consolidate your skills, do the following application exercise.

1. Identify one or more children who read at the third- or fourth-reader level.

2. Select appropriate reading material for a directed reading lesson.

3. Write a lesson plan that specifies your objectives and procedures for each segment of the lesson, including:

    a. teaching vocabulary

    b. eliciting past experiences

    c. establishing the purpose

    d. directed rereading

    e. extended activities

4. Teach the lesson in two sessions, allowing time for independent reading in between.

VOCABULARY

will enable you to

1. Diagnose students' needs for vocabulary instruction

2. Teach vocabulary using one of three methods—elements, or language-interaction pattern

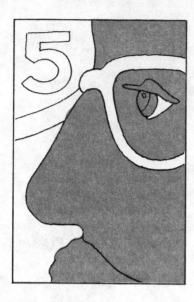

Ray Watson teaches reading to three groups at different reading levels. The group he is about to teach consists of eight gifted fourth graders who read at the sixth- and seventh-grade levels. For them, decoding is no problem. They can decode anything, even material they do not understand.

Today, Ray has a delightful poem for them to read but he anticipates problems. The poem contains many words the children may not know. If he lets them read it without prior instruction, the humor may pass over their heads. But if he belabors the poem too much, they could easily be turned off by an overdose of schoolmarmishness. In addition, there isn't much time. The children in the other reading groups are in the same room doing seatwork. Their attention span is short, which limits the time Ray can spend with the high group. The whole lesson must be finished in twenty minutes or less. This leaves less than five minutes at the beginning of the lesson for vocabulary and concept building.

The poem is reprinted below. What would you do to teach vocabulary in that opening five-minute period?

Which words and concepts should you teach?

_____   _____   _____

_____   _____   _____

_____   _____   _____

_____   _____   _____

_____   _____   _____

How would you teach them? (List the steps.)

_____

_____

_____

_____

_____

_____

_____

_____

_____

_____

THE SYMBIOTIC TRAGEDY OF PHOEBE THRACE

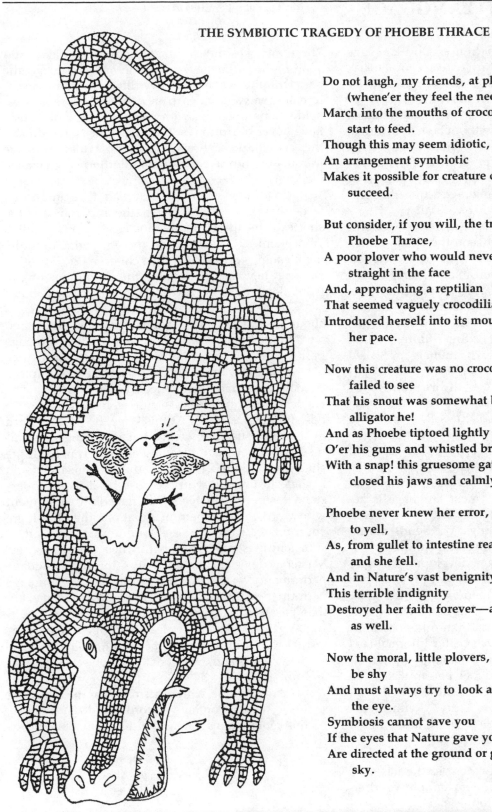

Do not laugh, my friends, at plovers who
    (whene'er they feel the need)
March into the mouths of crocodiles and boldly
    start to feed.
Though this may seem idiotic,
An arrangement symbiotic
Makes it possible for creature coexistence to
    succeed.

But consider, if you will, the tragic fate of
    Phoebe Thrace,
A poor plover who would never look her friends
    straight in the face
And, approaching a reptilian
That seemed vaguely crocodilian,
Introduced herself into its mouth, not slackening
    her pace.

Now this creature was no crocodile, but Phoebe
    failed to see
That his snout was somewhat broader—yes, an
    alligator he!
And as Phoebe tiptoed lightly
O'er his gums and whistled brightly,
With a snap! this gruesome gator
    closed his jaws and calmly ate her.

Phoebe never knew her error, and she vainly tried
    to yell,
As, from gullet to intestine realms, she tumbled
    and she fell.
And in Nature's vast benignity
This terrible indignity
Destroyed her faith forever—and her wretched self
    as well.

Now the moral, little plovers, is that you must not
    be shy
And must always try to look at folks directly in
    the eye.
Symbiosis cannot save you
If the eyes that Nature gave you
Are directed at the ground or gazing idly at the
    sky.

VOCABULARY AND LANGUAGE ACQUISITION

Understanding how children acquire language outside school will help you learn to teach vocabulary. Consider the fact that children usually acquire far more language before they even start school than they acquire at any other time in their lives. The fact that all children learn their language without benefit of formal instruction and with no apparent strain is a sobering object lesson. It contrasts sharply with the fact that not all children learn to read, even with great amounts of formal instruction. Informal language acquisition provides a useful model for teaching vocabulary.

Briefly, informal vocabulary acquisition is often a product of the interaction between the child and his mother. The interaction begins with an experience. For example, the child may see a small, furry brown animal and ask, "What's that?" His mother then functions as a verbal mediator for the experience. "That's a kitty," she says. The child accepts this word into his vocabulary as a useful label. His first intuitive notion may be that small, furry brown animals are called "kitty."

While on another outing with his mother, the child sees another small, furry brown animal. He labels it for his mother, "That's a kitty." But his mother corrects him, "No, that's a doggie." Gradually, the child learns to generalize correctly about cats and dogs, applying the label only when it is appropriate.

This anecdote illustrates several principles of language development. First, most language is acquired through verbal interaction with "significant others," such as parents, siblings, or friends during normal, everyday experience. Second, children probably vary in their language development more through differences in previous language interactions than through differences in experience. For example, many children may go to the zoo, but some will benefit much more from the experience than others because their mother or father is a much better informal language teacher. Third, meaning acquisition is gradual. A child's initial grasp of a word may be simplistic, like that of the child in the example, who thought that all small, furry brown animals were "kitty." Refinements in meaning are acquired more slowly than the initial label, often through trial and error.

Children do a surprising amount of intuitive language analysis. This is most evident in the mistakes they make as they learn to talk. For example, children may make statements similar to these:

"Daddy goed to the store."

"He gotted a new toy."

"That cup is mines."

"His foots are hurted."

These mistakes indicate that children assimilate and analyze the language they hear in order to extract the basic grammatical rules. They then use their own internally generated rules to produce original sentences, boldly experimenting with variations they obviously have never heard to test their usefulness. Gradually, they learn the exceptions to the general rules they have formulated intuitively and modify their language accordingly.

Children's errors indicate another important fact—that they are sensitive to the importance of the shortest meaningful phonological units (called "morphemes"), such as *-ed* and *-es*—which modify the meanings of words. When children err, it is often because they are generalizing the use of meaningful word elements to new words in a very rational way.

There is a difference between what children *know* about language (called "language competence") and what they actually *do* with language (called "language performance"). This difference is related to the degree of word mastery the child has attained. For example, a child may begin his experience with the word *round* by vaguely understanding its most common use—as a description of a shape. At this stage, he has the word in his linguistic competence but may be easily confused when a variant meaning of *round* is used. If the child had acquired cautious adult habits, he would hesitate to use the word because he doesn't understand it very well. Instead, children boldly experiment with words, using them in situations they think are appropriate. Through trial and error, they attain sufficient mastery of words for their own purposes. Mastery comes through activity—through language performance—rather than passivity. Active language performance, therefore, is a better indicator of mastery than passive language competence.

Virtually all language learning appears to be contextual. Children learn language informally by hearing new words spoken in relation to objects or events and unfamiliar words spoken together with familiar words. For example, a little girl may hear the following sentence, which contains a word she doesn't know. As this sentence is spoken, the child may obtain con-

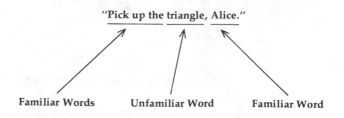

"Pick up the triangle, Alice."

Familiar Words   Unfamiliar Word   Familiar Word

textual information from the speaker's tone of voice and facial expression. She may pick up more clues from the speaker's interaction with the object if, for example, the speaker points to the triangle. And from the verbal context, Alice knows intuitively that the unfamiliar word is a noun and that it refers to some object she is capable of lifting. From this interaction of verbal contextual information, Alice may very well intuit the meaning of the new word.

These few principles of language acquisition are basic guides for teaching vocabulary. If planned instruction is similar to the informal processes that worked so well, it is reasonable to believe that the child's vocabulary will increase. The principles of language acquisition that should guide vocabulary teaching are:

1. Most word meanings are learned through moderated experience with a significant other.

2. Mastery of new words requires a process of verbal trial and error.

3. Vocabulary learning, unlike some other language learning, is a lifelong process.

4. Children are sensitive to the meanings of separable elements within words.

5. Contextual information surrounding unfamiliar words is useful in acquiring meaning.

A TEACHING STRATEGY

The teaching strategy presented in this chapter begins with diagnosis, which normally occurs a day or two before the actual vocabulary lesson. Next, the chapter describes how to plan vocabulary instruction using three different methods: (1) the *context pattern*, (2) the *word-elements pattern*, and (3) the *language-interaction pattern*. Finally, the chapter describes how to implement the strategy in the regular classroom just before and just after children read the intended selection. Even though actual vocabulary instruction is done very quickly, there are many specifics for your instruction to have maximum effect.

The first step in teaching vocabulary for reading is to determine the words that must be taught. Begin by examining from the child's point of view the reading material you plan to use. Try to identify in advance the potentially troublesome words. As a second criterion, try to select words that are vital to understanding the reading material. If a word may be troublesome to the child but is not essential to understanding the content, you may choose to leave it out of your instructional plan.

Turn back to the poem presented in the introduction to this chapter, "The Symbiotic Tragedy of Phoebe Thrace." The words that are both potentially troublesome for children and vital to understanding are these:

1. plovers	4. symbiosis	9. coexistence
2. tragic fate	5. introduced	10. indignity
3. gullet	6. vaguely	11. benignity
4. intestine	7. crocodilian	

Be especially alert for words that are common but are used in divergent ways. For example, the word *introduced* would appear to be easy. But it is used in the following way: ". . . introduced herself into its mouth, not slackening her pace." In this sentence, *introduced* means "entered into." The child may think he knows what it means when, in fact, he does not. Divergent word meanings like this must be taught.

After selecting the troublesome vocabulary, the next task is to determine whether or not each child needs instruction. For older children who read quite well, a paper-and-pencil inventory is useful. For younger children, diagnosis must often be verbal. In either case, the basic pattern for diagnosis is the same, whether it is presented orally or in writing. First, present the word in a sentence, preferably one that contains little contextual information. For the word *symbiotic*, the following model sentence would be appropriate: "The arrangement was *symbiotic*." Then ask the child to define the word: "What does *symbiotic* mean?" Next ask the child to give some examples: "Tell me about some things that were *symbiotic*."

If the child has not acquired prior verbal mastery of this word, he will not be able to define it or give examples. In this event, he definitely needs vocabulary instruction to learn it. If the child is able to define the word as it is used in the story, or if he gives examples similar to the word use in the story, he needs no instruction.

Figure 8-1 shows a paper-and-pencil inventory that can be used to determine children's instructional needs. (The inventory should include an item for each word in the list of words to be taught.)

After determining which words each child does or does not know, it is useful to make a vocabulary scoring grid. The chart in Figure 8-2 is appropriate for recording the results from a diagnostic inventory. The chart can then be used to control group interaction while teaching. This is helpful in vocabulary teaching since children who have prior mastery of a particular word tend to dominate teacher-child interaction, crowding out the possibility that those who need instruction will get it. The chart can be used as follows:

1.   As you teach a reading group, refer to the chart to determine who needs instruction for each word and who doesn't.

2.   Deliberately maximize interaction with those who need help and minimize interaction with those who don't.

3.   After those who need instruction have received it, allow those who don't need instruction a chance to have their say.

(If you use charts regularly, they may also be used to record skills attainment and to report such gains to the

───── figure 8-1 ────────────────────────────────

A DIAGNOSTIC VOCABULARY TEST

1. He saw some *plovers*.

   What are *plovers*? _____

   _____

   Where would one find *plovers*? _____

   _____

2. She met a *tragic fate*.

   What is a *tragic fate*? _____

   _____

   Give an example of a *tragic fate*. _____

   _____

3. It is in the *gullet*.

   What is a *gullet*? _____

   _____

   Where would one find a *gullet*? _____

   _____

4. It was an *indignity*.

   What is an *indignity*? _____

   _____

   Give an example of an *indignity*. _____

   _____

children's parents.) After diagnosis and charting, the next step is active teaching.

Patterns of Vocabulary Teaching

To teach vocabulary well, you will need to learn patterns of teaching that are consistent with children's intuitive strategies for acquiring language. The rub is that your teaching methods must do what informal acquisition processes did in much less time. Remember that in the normal reading lesson there are about five minutes for active vocabulary teaching.

Recall that the original problem was to teach vocabulary essential for understanding the poem "The Symbiotic Tragedy of Phoebe Thrace" to a small group of able readers. The words identified by the teacher as potentially troublesome were: *plovers, tragic fate, gullet, indignity, intestine, vaguely, introduced, benignity, coexistence,* and *symbiosis.* Diagnosis has indicated that some of the children need help on each of the words. The basic patterns of vocabulary teaching presented below refer back to the poem reproduced at the beginning of the chapter.

The Context Pattern. The context pattern is useful for teaching word meaning under certain conditions. First, the child should have sufficient decoding skill to produce a reasonable approximation of the unfamiliar word. If he can do this, he can then use contextual information to derive meaning. If he cannot approximate the word through decoding, he should receive the necessary instruction to do so before proceeding with vocabulary instruction. The second condition is that the unfamiliar word must be surrounded by several good contextual clues. If such clues are lacking, the word should be taught by some other method.

There are three steps in using the context pattern to teach vocabulary:

1. (Preparation) Identify words that have several contextual clues in the planned reading selection.

2. (Teaching) Point out the unfamiliar word to the children and tell them that the word is surrounded with clues to its meaning. Ask them to identify the contextual clues and explain the relationship to the unfamiliar word.

figure 8-2

A SCORING GRID FOR VOCABULARY

VOCABULARY WORDS

KEY:

0 = Prior mastery. No instruction needed.

/ = Needs instruction.

X = Attained mastery after instruction.

3.   (Teaching) If the children have difficulty, prompt them in identifying clues and explain the relationship of the clue to the meaning of the word.

In "The Symbiotic Tragedy of Phoebe Thrace," there are four words that should be taught by the context pattern: *plovers, tragic fate, gullet,* and *intestine.* Each of these words is surrounded by several contextual clues, which will aid in determining meaning.

To begin teaching (step two), write *plover* on the board and say, "Find this word in the poem. See if you can find some clues to its meaning in the words or pictures nearby." The children might say that a plover is something capable of marching and, therefore, is obviously alive and legged. Also, it is small enough to "march into the mouths of crocodiles." They might also notice that there is a picture of a bird at the top of the page. A plover, therefore, is a little bird.

If the children do not identify these clues to meaning, you may wish to prompt them (step three), perhaps by asking the following questions:

> **"Can you tell what a plover is from its actions?"**
>
> **"How big do you think a plover is from what you read?"**
>
> **"Are picture clues helpful in finding out what a plover is?"**

As children begin to use contextual clues successfully, you may decide not to give instruction for unfamiliar words prior to reading if the words are surrounded by obvious information in context. In this way, you would provide children with opportunities to develop habits of using context to discover meaning.

The Word-Elements Pattern. The word-elements pattern is useful for teaching the meaning of words that contain meaning-bearing parts, such as affixes (*un-* and *de-*) and easily recognizable root words (un-*break*able, im*press*). The problem with using word elements as clues to meaning is that one element may have several different meanings, such as the *de* in *de*-throne, *de*fuse, and *de*base. Or the element may have been absorbed into a word over the centuries and hence lost its original, separable meaning. Perhaps this is the case with *de* in *de*cide or *de*clare.

The inconsistent nature of word-element meanings makes it much easier for things to go wrong than to go right in teaching. For example, one way to go wrong is to teach children the meaning of an element that applies in only a few cases. Still another way of going wrong is to tell children to "look for the little word in the big word." This practice results in finding "little words" like *dig* in *indignity,* a very erroneous clue to meaning.

One way to go right in teaching meaning through word-element clues is to follow these steps:

1.   (Preparation) Select words for teaching by the word-elements pattern carefully. Make sure the elements to be taught have separable meanings and that this meaning is applicable to other words.

2.   (Preparation) Make a list of other words that contain the same element used in the same way.

3.   (Teaching) Present the same meaningful element in another word not found in the selection to be read. Tell the children what the element means in that word.

4.   (Teaching) Now write the word to be taught from the reading selection on the board. Ask the children to determine what the word probably means. To do this, they must generalize the knowledge they have acquired to a new situation.

The following is a sample application related to the original teaching problem. In "The Symbiotic Tragedy of Phoebe Thrace," there are three words that are suitable for teaching by the word-elements method (step one). The words are:

*sym*biotic   *co*existence   *in*dignity

These words are suitable for teaching by the word-elements method because each contains an element with a separable meaning.

The next step (step two) is to list other words that use the same element in the same way:

sym	*biotic*
(Means "together with")	(Means "of or related to life")
sym̲metrical	anti<u>biotic</u>
sym̲pathetic	sym<u>biotic</u>
sym̲biotic	

co	*in*
(Means "with" or "together")	(Often means "negation")
<u>co</u>inhabit	<u>in</u>ability
<u>co</u>author	<u>in</u>accurate
<u>co</u>incidence	<u>in</u>active
<u>co</u>existence	<u>in</u>congruent

The next step (step three) is to tell the children what the element means in a word similar to the one in the story:

> *sym:* "In *symmetrical, sym* means 'together' and *metrical* refers to measurement."

Another example:

> *co:* "In *coinhabit, co* means 'together' and *inhabit* refers to where one lives."

The last step (step four) is to ask the children to generalize meaning from the known word to the unfamiliar word:

> **"If you know what *sym* means in *symmetrical* and what *biotic* means in *antibiotic*, what do you think *symbiotic* might mean?"**

Another example:

> **"If you know what *co* means in *coinhabit*, what do you think *coexistence* means?"**

This instructional pattern encourages children to generalize the meaning of word elements to new words. This pattern is similar to what children do with word elements as they learn to talk.

If you wish to follow the experimentation aspects of language acquisition, you may add one more step. This step involves generating original uses for a language element. Children will enjoy combining new word elements with familiar words in the following way:

Original Word	Logical Meaning
symtelephone	To telephone together (obviously)
symbicycle	To bicycle together
symcreate	To create together

Again, be cautious. Word elements are clues to meaning but are often misleading for two reasons. First, elements usually have more than one meaning. Second, some word elements no longer have a separable meaning. Thus, your statements must reflect this uncertainty and tentativeness. The word-elements method is most useful for showing meaningful similarities, not for teaching constant meanings.

The Language-Interaction Pattern. The language-interaction method is useful for teaching almost any word. It is the same as the interaction the child often has with his out-of-school "language teachers." The language-interaction method is based on the assumption that the child has probably had the necessary experience to understand most words. But the child has not had sufficient language interaction at the time of the original experience to learn the words that pertain to the experience.

This method begins with a verbal probe to identify a previous experience related to the word. Then, through interaction, the label is applied to the previous experience. Finally, the child is asked to try out the new word, to test it for applicability to other similar situations or experiences.

The language-interaction pattern has five steps:

1. (Preparation) Identify words in the reading selection that are essential for meaning and not suitable for teaching by the context or word-elements patterns.

2. (Preparation) Plan for the interaction by imagining a common experience the child may have had that exemplifies the meaning of the word.

3. (Teaching) Ask the child to recall a suitable previous experience and to describe it briefly.

4. (Teaching) Label that experience with the new word.

5. (Teaching) Ask the child to tell about other situations to which the word may be applied.

In "The Symbiotic Tragedy of Phoebe Thrace," there is a word and an expression that should definitely be taught by the language-interaction method (step one). These are: *vaguely crocodilian* and *introduced. Vaguely crocodilian* refers to the appearance of the alligator. If the child does not understand this expression, he misses the reason for Phoebe's terrible error. *Introduced* in the poem means "to enter into." If the child doesn't know this, he misses the important fact that Phoebe walked right into the alligator's mouth. Understanding these two concepts is vital for comprehension.

The child is then asked to recall an appropriate experience (steps two and three). For *introduced,* the following query would be appropriate: "Have you ever walked into a place where you've never been before? Tell me about it." Perhaps the child will say that he walked into a paint store for the first time yesterday. This experience is suitable for labeling. You might say: "We can say that you *introduced* yourself into the paint store" (step four). After labeling, ask the child to generalize to a new situation (step five): "Tell about another time when someone *introduced* themselves into a new situation." When the child can do this and when he can generalize the use of the word to new situations, he has probably attained sufficient mastery of word meaning to understand it in the reading selection.

AN APPLICATION EXERCISE   Up to now you have been reading about vocabulary diagnosis and teaching. But there is an important difference between reading about vocabulary teaching and actually learning to do it. To operationalize your knowledge, do the following application exercise.

1.   Select a story you plan to use for reading comprehension a few days in advance.

2.   Make a list of the words the children might not understand.

3.   Write a diagnostic inventory for word meaning from the list of words. At least a day before the children read the story, administer the inventory and record the results on a scoring grid.

5.   Decide which teaching pattern is most appropriate for each word on the list and mentally plan the teaching steps.

6.   Just before the children read the story, teach the words suitable for the word-elements and language-interaction patterns in five minutes or less.

7.   As you teach, use the information from the scoring grid to help you direct instruction toward those who need it and avoid being dominated by those who do not need instruction.

8.   Now have the children read the intended selection.

9.   After children have read the story, use the context method to review the remaining words on your list.

Once you have acquired these skills, you will have attained above-average competence in teaching vocabulary. Your skill will benefit many children who are having trouble with reading comprehension. You will be able to diagnose one important aspect of their problem and give them suitable instruction, not only during the normal reading period but also during science, social studies, and mathematics.

ADVANCED COMPREHENSION: DISCUSSIONS

will enable you to

1. Maximize student talk and minimize teacher talk
2. Encourage the active participation of each child
3. Increase high-level comprehension skills

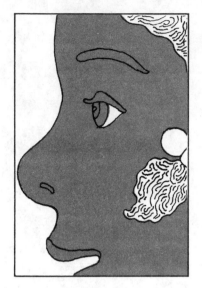

Nancy Allwood hates leading discussions. Even though she has done it many times, she still experiences discomfort and anxiety. Sometimes the children simply don't say anything, leaving her feeling embarrassed and inadequate. At other times, a few big-talkers monopolize the conversation, crowding out others who might like to talk. Then there are times when her children seem to answer each question in monosyllables. And the whole thing becomes a game of twenty-questions—not a discussion at all, just a recitation.

Nancy wonders whether it is worth the effort to try to hold discussions. Other activities such as written comprehension questions seem to require more thought and effort from the children and don't involve any agony on her part. Nancy is tempted to forget about discussions altogether.

How would you describe the problem? _____

_____

_____

_____

What would you do about it? _____

_____

_____

_____

Nancy Allwood's experiences with discussion are familiar to most experienced teachers. Certain children do sometimes monopolize the conversation, give trivial answers, or simply "clam up." The solution to these problems is to know how to *plan* a discussion in ways that will head off trouble and how to *lead* a discussion in ways that will resolve other problems as they arise. There are specific techniques for accomplishing both these objectives. Because the teacher must lead discussions several times a day in various content areas, developing your skill as a discussion leader will affect your students' learning and your own feelings about teaching. This chapter contains specific suggestions for planning and leading discussions, regardless of the content area.

THE PURPOSES AND CHARACTERISTICS OF DISCUSSIONS

The purpose of a discussion is to have a mutual exchange of views. Ideally, participants in a discussion voice their own opinions and listen to the opinions of others. As a result of this process, participants may modify their own opinions somewhat and see the issues in a new perspective. A good discussion is one that accomplishes the purposes just stated. One can generally tell whether a discussion is good or not simply by sitting and listening to it. First, a good discussion includes everyone both as a contributor and as a listener. Second, each person's comments are usually related to the previous speaker's comment. Third, participants often talk about issues in new and unexpected ways. Fourth, participants tend to lose their self-consciousness and become caught up in the issues. As you listen to a good discussion, you often feel yourself being drawn into it.

A poor discussion is even more obvious. It is usually dominated by a few members of the group, excluding the other members. Comments are often unrelated to the point made by the previous speaker—an unfortunate result of not listening. In a poor discussion, participants are often inhibited and self-conscious and hesitate to voice their true feelings and opinions. Other telltale signs are a high incidence of clichés and a low incidence of original comments. As you listen, you feel a growing annoyance and an urge to walk away.

Good discussions are an aid in teaching reading comprehension. The usual teaching procedure is to introduce a story, allow the children time to read it, and then lead a discussion of the story. The discussion process is intended to foster reading comprehension by reinforcing memory and teaching children to think of what they read in new and productive ways. Thus, learning to plan and lead discussions well will enable you to teach reading comprehension effectively. And, teaching discussion skills for their own sake will enable children to participate effectively in discussions of many kinds.

TECHNIQUES FOR HOLDING EFFECTIVE DISCUSSIONS

Finding Good Materials

The first job is to find good materials. If you want to have good discussions, find materials that are worth discussing. Stories related to real-life problems are excellent. All children experience emotional problems—feelings of rejection, loneliness, anger, powerlessness, and frustration. Children also experience dramatic upheavals in their lives—moving, family financial upsets, death, divorce, or illness. Children, like adults, are affected by current social problems, such as discrimination, poverty, inflation, crime, and unemployment. Further, children are often interested in momentous events—space flights, political elections, scientific discoveries, and catastrophes. If the topic is personally significant to the child, a successful discussion is a real possibility.

Readability is another consideration. The material used for discussion should not present many problems in word recognition for children in the discussion group. If children are using basal readers, conduct an informal reading inventory to ensure that the level is appropriate. When using library materials, you may wish to test children on a short excerpt to make sure that the level is not too high.

The length of the selection must also be considered. Literary discussion requires that children remember considerable information from their reading. Thus, you may wish to begin your discussion sessions with very short selections, gradually increasing the length until you achieve full book length.

"Children of Hong Kong" is an example of a story that follows these guidelines. The story is socially significant because it concerns income disparities among nations, the effects of population density, and cultural differences. The story is personally significant for children because they all have home responsibilities of various kinds. The story is reprinted in full below.

CHILDREN OF HONG KONG

A little Chinese girl in a pink flowered jacket and trousers came running along the street, her bright clothes fluttering around her frail body. In her hand she held a packet of postcards. There was a charming, hesitant smile on her face.

"Would you like to buy some postcards?" she asked, holding them up. The bright-colored photographs on the cards were of the beautiful Tiger Balm Gardens of Hong Kong, which were nearby.

"These are very good—good pictures of the gardens," she added. "And they cost only three Hong Kong dollars."

Wherever I had gone in Hong Kong, children had come running just as this little girl did. Mostly they had things to sell: beads and mangoes and colored slides of the city—pictures of the teeming harbor filled with luxury liners and freighters and junks and sampans, pictures of cable cars going up Victoria Peak, almost two thousand feet above the city, and pictures of the breathtaking view from the top of the peak. Every child seemed to be either selling something or working for his family. Even boys and

From The Old-Fashioned Ice Cream Freezer, *The SRA Reading Program, Level J. Copyright 1967, 1971, Science Research Associates, Inc. Reprinted by permission of the publisher.*

girls no older than five or six did their part by carrying small babies strapped to their backs.

"Only three Hong Kong dollars for the postcards," the girl repeated. "It is very little."

Her English was perfect. As she waited for me to make up my mind, she looked around quickly, perhaps already seeking another customer.

"You speak very good English," I said. "Where did you learn your English? Who taught you?"

The girl blinked shyly and tossed her straight black hair. "My teacher in school," she replied.

"And why aren't you in school today?"

"It is my turn to go to school in the afternoon," she answered. Suddenly she assumed a very businesslike manner; her face became serious.

"You want to buy my postcards?" she asked again.

"Yes, I do. But don't you go to school in the morning, too?"

"No," she said. "Some of the children go to school in the morning and some go in the afternoon. But not everyone can go to school. There is not enough room."

"How old are you?"

"Eleven," she said. Then I gave her the three Hong Kong dollars (worth about sixty cents in American money), and she handed me the postcards. There was a broad smile on her face now.

"Thank you," she said.

"Thank you."

"Goodbye," she said.

"Goodbye."

And then she was gone.

One afternoon a few days later I took a sightseeing bus tour of Hong Kong, the city whose name means "fragrant harbor" in Chinese. Over three million people live there, almost all of them Chinese. In recent years the population of this city on the southern coast of China has swelled enormously as refugees from other parts of China have sought homes. Many of those who want to live in Hong Kong have had to return to Communist China because they entered the city illegally, but each day the British government, which rules Hong Kong as a crown colony, allows some of the newcomers to remain. As a result, the streets of the hilly city are overflowing with people. In downtown areas, buses and streetcars and automobiles add their noises to the cries of the tradesmen and street peddlers. The sidewalks are crowded with shoppers and pedestrians. Wherever you look, the flow of life goes on and on.

With so many people in Hong Kong, there is not enough decent housing. Almost 400,000 people live in squatters' shacks or in flimsy rooftop homes. Row after row of apartment buildings have been built by the British government, but many people—140,000 in all—live on boats in the harbor. Everywhere children seem to chatter and play—and work.

The sightseeing bus took us to a V-shaped inlet so filled with boats that the water was hidden from view. Planks linking boat to boat served as streets. People ran back and forth over them, carrying goods and food. As soon as the bus stopped, groups of children crowded round it, looking for some small offering of money. There was a pleading look on their faces. Everybody wondered if there would ever be enough good housing and schools to take care of all these children. Some of them, the guide said, may never read a book in their lives.

In a section of the city called Aberdeen, on Hong Kong Island, I visited a beautiful floating restaurant that seemed out of place with all the poverty around it. To get to the restaurant, the tourists on the bus took a small sampan—a light boat with a curved cabin roof made of mats that were rolled partway up on one side. The boat could carry only six passengers at a time. Old women and young girls poled the sampan across the water to the restaurant, and then they returned for more passengers. A beautiful Chinese girl with a baby strapped to her back helped an older woman at the work of poling. Seated on a stool near them was a little boy about two years old. During the ride to the restaurant he did not speak or make a sound. Later he fell asleep behind one of the chairs.

From the upper deck of the floating restaurant you can watch the sampans bringing the tourists out to have their lunch. As each boat arrives, its deck is scrubbed clean by the women and girls. Then they return to shore. From time to time an older woman can be seen in a small boat bringing a basket to the workers on the sampans. In the basket are tiny cups of food—probably the raw fish and rice that are the chief diet of the people of Hong Kong.

In one of the sampans that day, a young girl was doing her schoolwork. She was kneeling on the floor of the boat, and her schoolbook was on the seat of a chair. She studied when she could. But she didn't have much time. When the boat had to leave on a trip, she quickly closed her book, put it in a safe place, and began to help pole the boat back to shore. Her young body strained against the pole while the older women steered the boat through the busy traffic of the harbor.

On the other side of the floating restaurant, young boys were diving for coins that tourists were tossing from their boat. Plunging into the murky and foul-smelling water to seize the coins, these boys were doing their part to earn a few pennies for their poor families.

At the end of the day I returned to the hotel, where a Chinese boy no more than fourteen or fifteen years old cared for my room. He brought a pot of hot tea, turned down the bed at night, and came to the room in a few seconds when I pressed the service buzzer. He was charming and cheerful, always working to make his life a little better—like so many of the children of Hong Kong.

Introducing the Story

Teachers may introduce each story by relating the content to be read to the students' previous experience. For example, if you wished to introduce the story "Children of Hong Kong," you might ask one of the following questions:

"Have you ever gone to a city that was *very* different from your own?"

"What do American children do to help their families?"

After eliciting the children's personal experiences, you must then be prepared to relate that experience to the story. For example, if the children respond well to the second question by describing duties they have at home, you could relate their experience to the story in the following manner:

Today your story is about a city where children live very differently from the way you do. This is a place where family life is different, school is different, and people have different attitudes about what children should do. As you read, compare their lives to your own and think of the similarities and differences.

The children then read the story silently.

Again, as you plan your story introductions, think of the two steps just described. First, elicit the children's previous experience. Second, relate the story to be read to those personal experiences.

Writing Discussion Questions

Provocative questions are another essential for good discussions. Much work has been done on questioning strategies for classroom use. Questions have been classified into categories on the basis of the mental operations that are required to answer them and ranked hierarchically. That is, the simpler types of questions are ranked lower, and the more complex types (requiring many mental operations) are ranked at the top of the hierarchy. For example, Carl Wallen has described eight different categories of questions and ranked them from the simplest to the most complex.[1] The categories are:

1. Recall-Identification — The child is asked to recall specific items that were directly mentioned in the selection.

2. Recall-Organization — The child is asked to organize specific items differently from the way they were presented in the story.

3. Interpretation-Summarization — The child is asked to identify the major idea presented in the entire selection or a designated section of it.

4. Interpretation-Conclusion — The child is asked to identify underlying ideas in an unstated cause-effect relationship that can be logically inferred from directly stated items in the selection.

5. Extrapolation-Consequence — The child is asked to use a previously identified cause-effect relationship to infer the consequence of changing either the cause or the effect item.

6. Extrapolation-Analogy — The child is asked to use a previously identified cause-effect relationship to infer what an analogous one might be.

7. Evaluation-Objective — The child is asked to make judgments about the reasonableness or soundness of statements or events in a selection based on an internal criterion, such as supporting evidence, reasons, or logic provided in the selection.

8. Evaluation-Subjective — The child is asked to make judgments about statements or events in the selection based on a criterion external to it, such as his own biases, beliefs, or preferences.

[1] Carl Wallen, *Competency in Teaching Reading* (Chicago: Science Research Associates, 1972).

This hierarchy is a useful guide for planning discussion questions. To plan a set of questions, first read the materials to be used for discussion. Then write one or several questions (however many seem appropriate) for each category related to the story. The questions can then be used to lead the discussion.

The following example may clarify the process. Suppose that you wish to plan a discussion for the story "Children of Hong Kong." After reading the story, write a list of discussion questions, as many questions for each category as seem logical and appropriate. For children at this reading level (high fourth- or fifth-grade equivalent), it is often helpful to ask enough questions from the lower categories so that they will recall the story as completely as possible and then to write questions for whichever of the higher categories seems appropriate. You might write a list similar to this:

Recall-Fact

1. Where did the story take place?

2. How is Hong Kong different from our city?

Recall-Organization

3. What were the jobs that the children of Hong Kong did?

4. What was a day in the life of a Hong Kong child like?

5. Why is Hong Kong so crowded?

Interpretation-Summarization

6. How could you describe the children in the story?

7. Describe the city in just one or two sentences.

Interpretation-Conclusion

8. Why do you think the Hong Kong children work so hard?

Extrapolation-Consequence

9. What do you think would happen if even more refugees came to Hong Kong?

10. What would happen if no more refugees came?

Extrapolation-Analogy

11. What other cities are like Hong Kong?

12. Are there any other children in other places who live or work like the Hong Kong children?

Evaluation-Objective	13. Is there anything in the story to indicate that the author really understands what life is like in Hong Kong?
Evaluation-Subjective	14. Is it good for the children of Hong Kong to work?
	15. If you were a tourist in Hong Kong, should you buy postcards from children?

After the children have read the selection, these questions can be used to guide the discussion. You can expect such a prepared list to result in a better discussion than a list prepared without regard to a hierarchy. The questions on the list require students to recall the story literally, to identify relationships among facts, and to evaluate various occurrences critically. Provocative questions like these also call for longer and more original responses from children than do simplistic questions. When children give original responses, their peers are more likely to listen to them and to relate their comments to what has just been said. In short, the use of a questioning strategy results in an authentic discussion rather than a recitation.

But there is more to learn. In addition to knowing how to plan for a discussion, you must also know how to conduct one.

Leading a Discussion

After everyone in the group has had ample time to read the selection, you may begin the discussion. Your role at this point is to ask the questions and to moderate the discussion in a way that will achieve its essential goals. Recognize that there are many potential pitfalls along the way. This section of the chapter reviews the essential goals of discussion, describes some common problems, and recommends procedures for alleviating the problems.

Your first goal is to maximize student talk and minimize teacher talk. It's not easy! If students are reluctant to speak, or if they are a little slow in formulating their answers, there is a strong temptation to tell them the answer. In this case, you are falling into the familiar trap of asking all the questions and then answering them. There are four ways to avoid this trap. First, start with questions from the simplest categories, especially those requiring literal recall of events in the story. Second, reinforce the children's correct responses with verbal praise and encouraging facial expressions. Third, allow ample time for the students to answer—even if there are some uncomfortable periods of silence. Fourth, if students cannot

answer important recall questions, tell them the approximate location of the information and ask them to find the answer in the selection and read it aloud. Your basic role in maximizing student talk is to be the "thought-jogger" and "emotional-support-leader" and to avoid being the "knower-and-teller-of-all-wisdom."

Your second goal is to get everyone into the discussion, to draw out the nonparticipants. You will need to identify nonparticipants and to control group interaction enough so that they have a chance to speak. Since you are chairing the discussion, you can direct some questions directly to the reluctant person. Also, you can reinforce them for speaking up. You may simply use praise or, better yet, build on their responses constructively. The following example illustrates these techniques:

(The children have finished reading "Children of Hong Kong" on the previous day. The teacher has begun the discussion and Mary is not participating.)

Teacher: "Mary, why do you think the children of Hong Kong work so hard?"

(Mary hesitates and several eager-beavers are bursting to answer, but the teacher simply ignores them, giving her a chance to formulate her answer.)

Mary: "I think it's probably because their parents don't have enough money."

Teacher: (Praises) "That's very logical." (To the group): "Why do you suppose that might be so?"

In the example, the teacher directed a question to Mary, gave her time to formulate her answer, praised her for her answer, and used it in a constructive way to further the discussion. If this procedure is repeated on other occasions, the teacher may reasonably predict that Mary will learn to participate in discussions.

Your third goal is to encourage children to think about their reading in new and productive ways. The use of questioning strategies alone will go far toward achieving this goal. But children will persist in using familiar, comfortable modes of thinking, rather than the more sophisticated ones you are attempting to encourage. Even on complex questions, children move toward "psychological closure" when they have formulated a minimal answer. For example, if you ask, "Why do you think the children of Hong Kong work so hard?" children are likely to answer the question as simply as possible and then to dismiss it. They might say, "Because they need the money," and be ready to forget about it because they have achieved closure.

Your job is to prevent them from reaching a psychological closure until they have thought about the question from a creative standpoint. For this particular question ("Why do you think the children of Hong Kong work so hard?"), the simplistic answer is not enough. They might think about the causes of economic necessity, about population density and the food supply, about supply and demand in the labor market, or about cultural expectations for children. Since this more sophisticated thinking is your goal, you may use a number of techniques to achieve it. You might simply rephrase the child's answer:

> **"Oh, they do it because they want the money for something."**

Or, you may ask for additional information:

> **"Tell me more about it."**

> **"Are there some other reasons?"**

Or, you may challenge their answer:

> **"Is it really that simple?"**

> **"But why do so many of them work?"**

> **"How do you know that?"**

You may choose to supply some new bit of information:

> **"Did you know that in overcrowded cities, children often do a great deal of work? Why do you think this is so?"**

Any of these devices will reopen a topic that has been settled too easily. By learning to recognize the symptoms of premature psychological closure and learning how to deal with it, you can teach your students to have more sustained, meaningful, and provocative discussions.

Finally, your fourth major goal is to teach children to value the contributions of their peers. Unfortunately, children often believe that the only person worth listening to is the teacher. This notion makes authentic discussion impossible. To participate in a discussion, it is essential that children learn to listen to other children. And if they are to be influenced by discussion, they must learn to value the insights made by other children.

There are several devices for teaching children to listen and value the contributions of their peers. These devices are used after one child has responded to a question. You may ask other children to repeat an answer:

> **"Let's see if everyone understood what Mary said. John, will you repeat her answer?"**

You may ask that the answer be rephrased:

> **"Pat, give Mary's answer in different words."**

You may ask for agreement or disagreement:

> **"Frank, do you agree with that answer?"**

You may ask the children to project the logical consequences of an answer:

> **"If this statement is true, what would it mean to other people?"**

You may ask other children to identify the merit in an answer:

> **"Why do you think that answer is such a good one?"**

Each of these devices requires that children listen to their peers and value what was said. Practicing all the other techniques described in this chapter will also help increase children's willingness to listen to each other. For example, if you minimize teacher talk, children will have more opportunities to hear each other's views. If you ask provocative questions, the views expressed will be more diverse than if you ask only simplistic recall questions and will also be more worthy of attention. And if you, the teacher, listen intently to what children say, use their responses to further discussion, and reinforce and support their discussion with your comments, mannerisms, and facial expressions—you will be teaching attentive listening and mutual respect through your personal example.

AN APPLICATION EXERCISE

Up to now, you have been reading about discussions. You have learned that discussions can be improved through using questioning strategies, selecting appropriate materials, and guiding discussions with specific techniques. To consolidate these skills, do the following application exercise.

1. Identify a small group of children who are reading on a similar level.

2. Select appropriate reading material for discussion.

3. Write a list of questions related to the reading material and based on the hierarchy presented in this chapter.

4. Introduce the reading selection to the children and allow them time to complete it.

5. Lead the discussion using the techniques described in this chapter.

6. Tape-record the discussion for later evaluation. When you listen to the recording, evaluate the discussion in relation to the goals stated in this chapter.

PERSONAL CONFERENCES

will enable you to

1. Motivate the child to do further reading

2. Produce diagnostic information for planning instruction

3. Impart necessary reading skills

4. Maintain a continuous record of progress

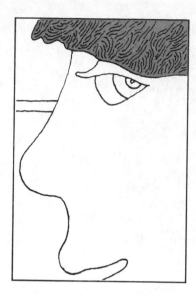

Theresa Allan uses a series of programmed, soft-cover books to individualize reading for her first and second graders. Since the books are self-instructional and self-scoring, there is little she needs to do while children work with them. The materials present each phonic element so gradually that many children can master each new skill simply by reading the material, choosing the correct response in each frame, and checking their responses against the answer key in the booklet's margin. Theresa spends most of her time supplying the occasional word children don't know or checking students' progress with intermittent tests.

Things had been going pretty well until recently, when children started to lose interest in their work. Instead of applying themselves, children have begun to dawdle and daydream. Other children work halfheartedly for a while and then find some excuse to stop. And there is never any better excuse to stop working than the nudge of a friend who wants to talk. In short, friendship is progressing in Mrs. Allan's room but reading is not.

John Hilling uses a multilevel kit to individualize reading in his fifth-grade class. His students like the kit because it has selection at their own reading levels, interesting stories, and moderate-to-easy exercises. John likes the kit because it seems to run itself, leaving him time to correct papers from other subjects or do other necessary tasks. John also thinks that the kit provides a good change of pace from the basal-reader program that is used during the rest of the school year.

But Mr. Hilling has just encountered an upsetting problem: his students are cheating. Instead of doing the exercises and self-scoring their work, they either self-score the exercises dishonestly or simply copy answers from the self-correction key cards without doing the work at all. In this way, several children have misled Mr. Hilling into promoting them to a higher reading level before they were ready. So the problem has compounded itself: children are cheating and consequently are finding themselves working at their frustration level.

Geri Miller has begun an individualized reading program with her third graders. She has set up a classroom reading center at the back of the room, featuring listening stations, reading games, magazines, and (most important) over 200 trade books. During reading, children are encouraged to visit the reading center, make a selection, and read whatever suits them best. Ms. Miller moves around the room, talking quietly with individual children and helping them with hard words.

Geri likes the program and so do her students. But there are problems. Geri knows that the program provides well for varying interests but she is unsure of its adequacy for developing children's phonic skills. She is also uncertain about the children's comprehension skills. She has not had time to read all the trade books in the center and so she usually feels at a loss in discussing the stories with the children. Her misgivings about skill development are growing stronger as parent-conference time approaches, since she wonders what she will tell the parents about their children's reading.

Each of these teachers is operating an individualized reading program. And each teacher has some unique problems and at least one problem in common. See if you can identify the unique and common problems.

What are the unique problems of each teacher?

Mrs. Allan: _____

Mr. Hilling: _____

Ms. Miller: _____

What is the common problem shared by all three teachers? _____

_____

_____

_____

_____

_____

What would you do about these problems? _____

_____

_____

_____

_____

_____

THE COMMON PROBLEM: LOSING TOUCH

The teachers in all three examples have lost touch with their children. In Mrs. Allan's and Mr. Hilling's rooms, the children have become alienated and apathetic because they interpret their teachers' lack of involvement with them as a sign of not caring. Ms. Miller's children are doing better, but there are still difficulties. She has lost touch with their reading skill needs. Geri Miller is heading for a series of poor parent-teacher conferences that will be long on vague generalities and short on specifics, because she has lost track of her students.

All three teachers are operating on the assumption that individualized reading programs run themselves. This is rather far from the truth. Granted, individualized programs require students to do many things for themselves that teachers normally do for them. In an individualized program, children often select stories, read them, follow directions, do exercises, score their own work, and chart their own progress. These are very high and worthy expectations for elementary children. However, children fulfill these expectations best when the teacher demonstrates great interest in their progress, awareness of their skill needs, and willingness to help them with difficulties. On the other hand, many children *cannot* fulfill these expectations when they are completely neglected. Consequently, the practice can result in severe classroom problems.

A regular schedule of reading conferences is vital to the success of almost any individualized reading program. Reading conferences head off the problems you have just read about. They provide an opportunity to diagnose and teach skills, to guide the selection of books, and to encourage good study habits. Furthermore, a reading conference is an opportunity to get to know each child as an individual.

In addition, children like having conferences. They appreciate the feeling that the teacher is paying complete attention to them and is interested in their problems, progress, and their personal feelings. Children often come away from a good reading conference with a new reading skill, a sense of direction, and a feeling of encouragement.

But all this depends on whether you know how to organize a series of conferences and know precisely what to say and do at each one. This chapter is designed to help you attain skill in conducting an effective series of reading conferences.

PREPARATION FOR THE READING CONFERENCE

Begin planning for a series of conferences by asking yourself what you wish to accomplish. Your reading conferences will, with careful planning, result in changes in student behavior. As a result of your efforts, students will be able to do something they couldn't or wouldn't do before. Clarifying your objectives in your own mind is a prerequisite for conducting effective conferences.

Formulating Instructional Objectives

Instructional objectives for the personal reading conference should be thought of in relation to degree of improvement rather than as an absolute standard. For example, here are some objectives that are useful in conducting conferences:

1. *Rate.* When placed in reading material at his instructional level, the child will demonstrate continuous improvement in oral reading, up to a rate of 140 words per minute.

2. *Work Habits.* The child will maintain any records required by the program with which he is working. The child will show a pattern of increasing productivity during the reading period.

3. *Skills.* The child will learn to decode any word within his speaking vocabulary.

4. *Book Selection.* When he goes to the school library or reading center, the child will select books at his independent or instructional reading level but not at his frustration level.

5. *Interests.* The child will select and read materials on topics in which he was not previously interested. Or, the child will read materials of increasing depth and complexity in areas in which he had a strong previous interest.

6. *Attitude.* The child will read more books and magazines than he previously did whenever time is available.

7. *Feelings About Reading.* The child will acquire and express feelings of well-being during the reading time.

This list of seven major objectives is actually too long for use with any one child. More reasonably, you may appraise each child's needs as you begin to work with him, decide on three or four major objectives, and focus on them. For example, if you are working with a child whose independent reading level is equivalent to a fifth-grade reader—but the child reads very few books and only on one topic and is also careless with his work—you would formulate your objectives accordingly. Conferences with him would focus on work habits, book selection, and interests.

The Conference Record Notebook

You will also need to develop an anecdotal record-keeping system for the personal reading conference. This record is indispensable since it is your only way of assessing a child's degree of progress toward your instructional objectives. Figure 10-1 is a sample page of a teacher's anecdotal record-keeping system.

To prepare a series of individual conferences with a group of children, duplicate at least one page of the Conference Record Notebook for each child. Enter each child's name on a separate page and put the pages together in a looseleaf notebook (Conference Record Notebook). This Conference Record Notebook may then be used as a guide and permanent chronicle of progress in conducting individual conferences. More detailed examples of entries in the Conference Record Notebook will be given later in this chapter.

Ensuring Order in the Classroom

The next preparatory step is to ensure relative order in the classroom while conferences are in session. For example:

1. Students must know that they will have their turns on a regular basis. Establish a schedule and announce who will have their conferences on that day. This eliminates some arm-wagging and pleas like "Can I be next?"

2. Minimize interruptions by encouraging students to seek help with unfamiliar words, on following directions, and so on from each other.

3. Select a location for conferences where you are out of the direct line of students' vision, but where you can see all!

4. Keep each conference short—from three to five minutes. Numerous short conferences are preferable to fewer, longer conferences.

When you have done these things, you are almost ready to have a productive series of personal reading conferences. But there are still some things you need to know: what, specifically, to say and do at each personal conference.

——— figure 10-1 ———

SAMPLE PAGE FROM THE CONFERENCE RECORD NOTEBOOK

Child's Name _____ Grade _____

Beginning Date _____ Ending Date _____

	Conference 1	Conference 2	Conference 3	Conference 4	Conference 5
Level					
Productivity					
Skills					
Interest					
Feelings					

THE PERSONAL READING CONFERENCE

The essential teaching purposes of the personal reading conference are to obtain diagnostic information, to teach skills at the precise point of need, and to motivate each child. The purposes can be accomplished only through a series of conferences directed toward specific objectives. During the first few conferences with each child, decide what you wish him or her to accomplish. During the subsequent conferences, direct the child's efforts toward those objectives by teaching the essential skills and reinforcing the behavior you think desirable.

The sections that follow illustrate what you might say and do to help your students attain the desired instructional objectives.

Reading Level

The first objective of an individualized reading program is for children to learn to select books or to maintain themselves (in the case of programmed materials) at a reading level of appropriate difficulty. The simplest way to assess whether each child is working at an appropriate level is to have him read a short passage aloud. Then determine the ratio of errors to words read correctly and compare this percentage to the following criteria:

Percentage for Word Recognition	Functional Reading Level
98% to 100%	Independent Reading Level
90% to 97%	Instructional Reading Level
89% or lower	Frustration Reading Level

Children usually work best in an individualized program if they are reading materials midway between the independent and instructional reading levels. At this level, children can function with little help from the teacher or from their friends, but there is still some challenge for reading development on each page.

Be directive if a child is obviously in materials at an inappropriate reading level. If the materials are highly structured, explain why you think he should be reassigned to a different level and then reassign him to that level. If the child is selecting trade books that are too difficult, teach him to select books at his level by counting the words he doesn't know on each page and then asking himself if he really understands the content. Help him to make better selections from the classroom reading center and, in the future, praise him for selecting books at an appropriate level.

Study Habits

The second essential goal of every reading conference is for children to acquire good study habits. Common objectives are for children to increase their productivity (read more books, do more exercises), avoid distraction, follow directions, and be neat. These objectives can be attained by using reinforcement techniques during reading conferences. To begin, decide what the child should learn to do. Then assess his present behavior: what is he doing right now in relation to the objective?

In the Conference Record Notebook, record a description of the child's present behavior. Next, explain to the child what you want him to do. During subsequent reading periods, observe his behavior to determine whether he is progressing and record appropriate observations in the notebook. When he comes for his next conference, let him read the positive comments you have recorded and praise him for each improvement.

For example, suppose that a child who is working in a series of programmed readers has begun to dawdle. Your objective is for him to get more done each day. To accomplish this objective, count the number of pages he does on a particular day and record this number in the Conference Record Notebook. Then explain to him that he needs to work harder. On subsequent days, record the number of pages he does and praise him for any improvement.

Skills

The personal reading conference can also be used to diagnose reading skills. The simplest way to do this is to listen to the child read aloud and note precisely in the Conference Record Notebook the types of errors he is making. This record of errors is then used as a guide for planning instruction.

The advantage of informal diagnosis during the reading conference is that teaching can follow immediately. For example, suppose the child makes the following error:

Text: "The stranger put both hands over his fine beard."

Child reads: "The standing . . . put both hands over his fine beard."

You would then note the substitution of *standing* for *stranger* in the Conference Record Notebook and quickly check for previous notations of similar substitution errors. If there is evidence of many similar errors, you may teach a mini-lesson on syllabication immediately. You may also assign an independent ac-

tivity for the child to do, such as a game, a tape-recorded exercise, or a workbook page that deals with the precise skill he needs to acquire. A description of these activities, the mini-lesson and the follow-up assignment, is entered in the Conference Record Notebook.

Interests

Perhaps you are concerned about children's ability to find reading materials that interest them. You would then find it useful to assess interests. Ask the child if he likes what he is now reading. If the child answers that he likes the book very much, you are onto something very important—a reading interest. Next, determine the approximate reading level of the book. This information, reading interest and general reading level, should be recorded in the Conference Record Notebook as a guide to helping the child select other books he will enjoy.

You may wish simply to capitalize on an existing interest to get the child to read more. In this event, use information about interests as a guide for selecting trade books the child will enjoy. If the child says he liked *Chitty-Chitty Bang-Bang*[1] because it was funny and exciting, he may enjoy similar books, such as *Homer Price*[2] or *Charlie and the Chocolate Factory*.[3]

But if your objective is to diversify and expand a child's reading interests, your approach would be different. You might ask the child about his life outside of school: Does he belong to any clubs? Is he taking some type of lesson? Which television programs does he enjoy? What does he want to be when he grows up? Does he have some personal concerns? This information may then be used to help the child select reading materials related to his real-life interests and concerns.

Feelings

The personal reading conference is also an ideal time to assess and improve a child's emotional orientation toward reading. Feelings of anxiety during reading periods and limitations imposed by their own self-concepts prevent many children from overcoming their reading-skill problems. Although the two factors are obviously interrelated, they will be discussed separately.

---

[1] Ian Fleming, *Chitty-Chitty Bang-Bang* (New York: Random House, 1968).

[2] Robert McCloskey, *Homer Price* (New York: Viking Press, 1943).

[3] Roald Dahl, *Charlie and the Chocolate Factory* (New York: Alfred A. Knopf, 1964).

Anxiety during reading is a product of past experience. In *I'm OK—You're OK*,[4] Harris asserts that anxiety-producing experiences from the past live on indefinitely in our subconscious minds. These subconscious memories result in hard-to-control general feelings of anxiety whenever conditions are similar to the original events that caused them. Consider what this means in relation to a child with a reading problem. For this child, almost every school assignment may have been an anxiety-producing situation. Each reading assignment was a struggle. And each follow-up discussion, a source of embarrassment and humiliation. This experience is then repeated during every class period, on every school day, throughout all his years of schooling. It is reasonable to believe that these experiences produce anxiety for the child every time he is asked to read.

In *Games People Play*,[5] Berne says that all of us talk to ourselves, and the message may be positive or negative. We play "tapes" (repetitious unspoken statements) over and over again, in certain situations, saying what we think of ourselves. Think what children who have experienced reading failure may be saying to themselves during reading:

"You're dumb!"

"You can't learn to read!"

"No one can teach you!"

"Reading is for girls, not boys!"

"Think about something else and they (teachers) won't bug you!"

"Teachers don't like me because I'm dumb."

"I'm not as good as other kids!"

This self-destructive pattern is integral to the self-concept the child is developing.

The self-concept is a product of messages one receives from "significant others," such as parents, brothers, sisters, friends, and teachers. These messages are internalized and adopted as our own. Therefore, what significant others tell us about ourselves becomes what we think we are. That is, the messages become our self-image. We think of ourselves as smart or dumb, pretty or ugly, graceful or clumsy, interesting or dull, likeable or unlikeable because of the messages we receive from these significant others.

Most poor readers have a negative self-concept. Part of this comes from the teacher—certainly a significant other in the life of a young child—who is disappointed in the child's failure to read in the early grades and, perhaps inadvertently, lets him know it. More negative messages come from the mother, who is also concerned and disappointed about the child's reading failure. Still other more direct and cruel messages come from brothers, sisters, and classmates: "You're really a dummy, John." Or, "John reads so slow I lose my place." All of this results in a self-concept of nonreader, slow-learner, dumbbell, or underachiever—and often to a related, compensating self-concept of class jester, tough-guy, or rebel.

Feelings of anxiety, futility, and inferiority must be alleviated if the child is to learn to read well. Your instructional objective is to enhance the child's self-image. You want him to believe different things about himself, to play "new tapes" such as:

"I can learn to read."

"I need to learn to read."

"My teacher likes and cares for me."

"My teacher knows how to help me."

"I am as good as other kids in some things, and better in a few things."

To attain this objective, begin by doing a little boasting. Tell the child, "I have helped other boys and girls with problems like yours." Or, "I know many special teaching methods that will help you." Also, explain to the child that most of the assignments you give him will be things he can do. And if they are not, you want to know about it.

Play your role as a significant other to the fullest. Do this by teaching him the skills he needs and praising him for mastering them. Do it by placing him in materials at his independent and instructional reading levels and by assuring him that you, too, read "lots of easy books." Notice and praise him when he is doing his work, reading more pages, or improving in fluency. And use the Conference Record Notebook to convince him that your positive statements are more truthful than the old, negative statements that he has been making to himself.

A CONTINUOUS RECORD OF PROGRESS

The Conference Record Notebook is your essential tool for convincing the child that the "new tapes" are, indeed, true. To explain, each time you confer

---

[4] Thomas A. Harris, *I'm OK—You're OK: A Practical Guide to Transactional Analysis* (New York: Harper & Row, 1969).
[5] Eric Berne, *Games People Play: The Psychology of Human Relationships* (New York: Grove Press, 1964).

with the child, you record in the notebook the child's progress toward attainment of specific objectives. Each time you confer, you also instruct the child in any needed skills and praise him for improvements. Under these conditions, children *do* progress and the entries in the Conference Record Notebook prove it. The evidence contained in the Conference Record Notebook can then be used to convince the child and his parents that he is learning to read. Children who have previously failed need a lot of convincing that things are getting better. And the combination of the written record, renewed optimism from parents, and encouragement and praise from you is very effective. Consistent and skillful use of the Conference Record Notebook is an absolute necessity. The next few pages explain how to make entries and use the notebook.

The following suggestions are useful for deciding what kinds of entries to make each day:

1.   Entries are consistent with the planned objectives and goals of instruction.

2.   Entries show whether or not the child is improving. Therefore, data about any behavior must be entered into the notebook repeatedly.

3.   Entries for any given day contain information related to several different behaviors.

4.   Entries must be intelligible to the child and his parents.

Here are three examples of entry systems for the Conference Record Notebook. Each example refers back to one of the teaching situations described at the beginning of this chapter.

Example One. Theresa Allan uses a series of programmed, soft-cover readers with her first- and second-grade children. Her instructional objectives may be stated as follows:

1.   Each child will begin work promptly at the beginning of the period and do as much as he can during the available time.

2.   Each child will show a pattern of increasing productivity during the reading period.

3.   Each child will mark his booklet without looking at the correction key, and then look at the key to check his own response.

4.   Each child will gradually increase his oral-reading fluency up to 140 words per minute.

5.   Each child will select and do reading activities from the reading activity center during his free time.

Mrs. Allan uses these objectives as a guide for conducting conferences and making entries in the

Conference Record Notebook. During the conference, Mrs. Allan determines how many pages the child will complete that day and records that information as an indicator of decoding fluency. She praises the child for any improvement in pages completed or number of words read. She also records the fact that the child faltered while reading words beginning with *wh* and *sh*. This information will be used to plan instruction. Finally, Mrs. Allan records the fact that the child had selected and read a library book and praises him for that.

Mrs. Allan's daily entries in the Conference Record Notebook follow a consistent format. Each block records a single conference. As time goes on and repeated entries are made, the records become increasingly useful. Mrs. Allan uses the records to prove to children that she does notice and care about their work and that they are improving in pages read, reading fluency, and books selected. When parents come for a conference, she will also use the record to reassure them that the child is working hard and is learning to read.

Example Two. Mr. Hilling uses a multilevel kit to individualize reading. His instructional objectives for most of his students may be stated as follows:

1.   Each child will follow the teacher's directions about scoring and record-keeping procedures.

2.   Each child will master reading skills he previously didn't have.

3.   Each child will select and read library books appropriate to his interests and reading level.

4.   Each child will comprehend story content in selections of increasing difficulty.

5.   Each child will write original stories related to the selections that interest him most in the reading kit.

Mr. Hilling uses these objectives as a guide for conducting conferences and making entries in the Conference Record Notebook. During each conference, Mr. Hilling examines the student's workbook to determine whether he is following directions well. He praises the student for neatness and accuracy and also points out any need for improvement. Next, he asks the child to read the first paragraph or two aloud. As the child reads, Mr. Hilling listens for any errors indicative of skill needs. If Mr. Hilling notices a skills problem, he often teaches a mini-lesson on the spot. Or, he records the skill needed in the Conference Record Notebook. Before he proceeds, John Hilling usually finds something to praise about the child's oral reading. Next, he asks the child if he liked the story. If the child liked the story, Mr. Hilling makes a note of the

──────── figure 10-2 ─────────────────────────────────────

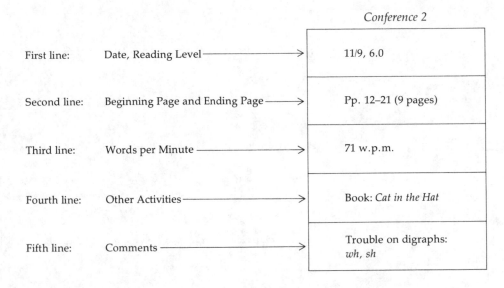

MRS. ALLAN'S DAILY ENTRIES

Conference 2

First line:	Date, Reading Level ⟶	11/9, 6.0
Second line:	Beginning Page and Ending Page ⟶	Pp. 12–21 (9 pages)
Third line:	Words per Minute ⟶	71 w.p.m.
Fourth line:	Other Activities ⟶	Book: *Cat in the Hat*
Fifth line:	Comments ⟶	Trouble on digraphs: *wh, sh*

──

general topic and reading level in the notebook. Later, he will use this information to help the child select a book he enjoys from the school library. If all has been going well in word recognition, Mr. Hilling concentrates on comprehension. How well did the child understand the key words in the selection? Did the child miss any comprehension questions? If so, what kinds of questions were they? Brief notes on problems or improvements in comprehension go down in the Conference Record Notebook. Finally, Mr. Hilling ends the conference with another word of encouragement.

The notes from this personal reading conference are shown in Figure 10-3. Notice that he uses a consistent format to indicate skill needs and improvements.

Here again, the records become more useful as repeated entries are made. Mr. Hilling uses the records to prove to each child that he does notice and care about the child's work. Mr. Hilling's habit of showing children their own records of improvement and praising them for each advance is tremendously motivating for his students, and his constant involvement with children as they work in the multilevel kit has greatly reduced the problem of cheating.

Example Three. Geri Miller has been running an individualized reading program based mainly on free selection of trade books. Her instructional objectives may be stated as follows:

1. Each child will select books appropriate for his reading level.

2. Each child will be continuously occupied with reading or reading-related tasks during the reading period.

3. Each child will master any word-attack skills when he encounters problems by obtaining help from another child or from the teacher.

4. Over a period of time, each child will read books of increasing difficulty and books about new topics.

5. Over a period of time, each child will develop a more positive self-image as a reader and develop a feeling of well-being while reading.

Ms. Miller uses these objectives as a guide for conducting conferences and making entries in the Conference Record Notebook. Geri begins each conference by determining whether the child has selected a book he can read. To do this, she asks the child to read a short passage aloud. If the child makes no more than one error in every twenty words, she assumes that the child has sufficient word-attack skills to read the book. If not, she usually advises him to select an easier book. At the same time, Geri listens for the specific kinds of errors the child makes and writes them down in the Conference Record Notebook. For children at the primary reading levels, she often teaches some skills during the conference. Geri praises the child for positive aspects of his oral reading and praises him even more for appropriate book selection. Next, Ms. Miller checks comprehension. If she is famil-

figure 10-3

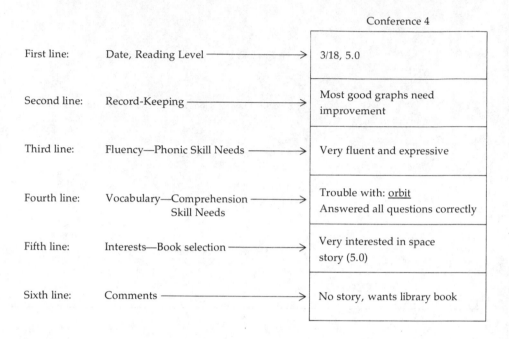

MR. HILLING'S DAILY ENTRIES

		Conference 4
First line:	Date, Reading Level ⟶	3/18, 5.0
Second line:	Record-Keeping ⟶	Most good graphs need improvement
Third line:	Fluency—Phonic Skill Needs ⟶	Very fluent and expressive
Fourth line:	Vocabulary—Comprehension Skill Needs ⟶	Trouble with: <u>orbit</u> Answered all questions correctly
Fifth line:	Interests—Book selection ⟶	Very interested in space story (5.0)
Sixth line:	Comments ⟶	No story, wants library book

iar with the book, she asks comprehension questions of several kinds. If the book is unfamiliar, she asks the child to summarize the story in several sentences and asks a few probing follow-up questions after that. Either procedure tells her whether the child has good general comprehension of the book. Again, she praises the child if he understands what he has read.

Ms. Miller also teaches children to obtain help when they need it. They are supposed to write down in a personal word book words they cannot pronounce or do not understand and ask a friend or the teacher for help. During the conference, she asks to see their word list—an indicator of whether they are, indeed, seeking help when they need it. She praises them if they have been doing so.

Finally, Ms. Miller talks to them about their feelings during reading. She assures them that they should feel good about themselves and that their efforts are resulting in improvements. She bolsters her assertion with the record of books read and problems overcome. Often, she finds something else to praise them for—a new shirt or dress, a kind thing they have done, or something special they have learned to do. Her reasoning in doing this is that students will perform better in school if they develop a positive self-image.

Ms. Miller keeps careful notes on each reading conference. A single entry is shown in Figure 10-4. She uses a consistent format related to her instructional objectives so that she can assess improvements.

As in previous examples, the records become more useful as repeated entries are made. Over a period of weeks and months, the records help Ms. Miller keep track of what her students are doing and the improvements they make. She can then use the records to demonstrate to the children and their parents that she knows and cares about her students' progress.

Other Applications

So far, this chapter has described how to plan and conduct personal reading conferences with three different types of individualized programs. Although the personal reading conferences were somewhat different in each case, the plan and basic premises were the same. Reading conferences are intended to keep the teacher continuously involved with the children. Conferences are a time to monitor children's progress, diagnose specific skill needs, teach new concepts, and motivate children. There will probably always be a need for personal conferences. Even though specific programs will change, children's need for close personal attention will not. Once you learn the basics of conducting a personal reading conference, you will be

────── figure 10-4 ──────────────────────────────────────

MS. MILLER'S DAILY ENTRIES

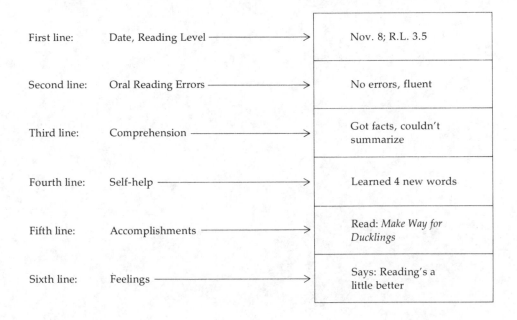

First line:	Date, Reading Level ⟶	Nov. 8; R.L. 3.5
Second line:	Oral Reading Errors ⟶	No errors, fluent
Third line:	Comprehension ⟶	Got facts, couldn't summarize
Fourth line:	Self-help ⟶	Learned 4 new words
Fifth line:	Accomplishments ⟶	Read: *Make Way for Ducklings*
Sixth line:	Feelings ⟶	Says: Reading's a little better

able to apply your skill and help children learn to read, no matter what type of individualized program you may use.

AN APPLICATION EXERCISE   Up to now, you have been reading about personal reading conferences. But there is an important difference between reading about conferences and actually learning to conduct them. To operationalize your knowledge, do the following application exercise:

1. Choose a set of materials designed for individualizing reading.

2. Decide just what you want your students to do as they work with the materials. List these objectives.

3. Make a Conference Record Notebook suitable for use in the series of planned conferences.

4. Teach your students how to use the individualized materials you have chosen.

5. Conduct a series of personal reading conferences with your students that will result in their attaining the instructional objectives.

6. Keep a continuous record of children's progress in a Conference Record Notebook.

7. Use the entries in the Conference Record Notebook to demonstrate to the child that he is learning to read.

8. Use the Conference Record Notebook to show the child's parents how much the child has improved.

APPENDIX: PAIRS TEST OF DECODING SKILLS

Child's Name _____ Grade _____

Examiner _____ Room Teacher _____ Date _____

Directions: Examiner says the first word in a pair and asks the child to say the second word. Any errors are recorded verbatim on the answer sheet.

SUBTEST A   Initial Consonants

1. toy-boy	12. sip-hip	23. hip-rip
2. fin-bin	13. lump-jump	24. cut-rut
3. tap-cap	14. tab-jab	25. cap-sap
4. sup-cup	15. dot-lot	26. mix-six
5. hot-dot	16. tap-lap	27. bell-tell
6. him-dim	17. rap-map	28. hip-tip
7. sun-fun	18. hill-mill	29. fin-win
8. sell-fell	19. nub-nib	30. tell-well
9. tap-gap	20. get-net	31. nip-yip
10. sob-gob	21. kin-pin	32. jell-yell
11. cut-nut	22. bat-pat	

From An Ounce of Prevention Plus a Pound of Cure © 1977 Goodyear Publishing Company, Inc.

SUBTEST B Final Consonant

1. pit-pin
2. rug-run
3. bet-bed
4. sap-sad
5. bat-bag
6. rip-rig
7. fan-fat
8. leg-let
9. sit-sip
10. sod-sop
11. hip-him
12. rag-ram
13. peg-pen
14. ram-ran
15. bit-bib
16. lag-lab

SUBTEST C Middle Short Vowels

1. fix-fox
2. dug-dog
3. bad-bid
4. hop-hip
5. pin-pen
6. lot-let
7. cap-cup
8. fin-fun
9. him-ham
10. rut-rat

SUBTEST D Middle Long Vowels and Vowel Digraphs

1. ran-rain
2. plan-plain
3. dim-dime
4. slid-slide
5. hat-hate
6. scrap-scrape
7. bed-bead
8. sell-seal
9. cost-coast
10. got-goat
11. fond-found
12. shot-shout
13. shot-shone
14. spot-spoke
15. blot-blow
16. slop-slow

SUBTEST E Initial-Consonant Blends and Digraphs

1. ring-thing
2. bud-thud
3. tip-whip
4. file-while
5. hop-shop
6. tell-shell
7. till-chill
8. burn-churn
9. bag-flag
10. stop-flop
11. kid-slid
12. bed-sled
13. clip-skip
14. fin-skin
15. ham-swam
16. dim-swim
17. hem-stem
18. hop-stop
19. slip-drip
20. bum-drum
21. flap-trap
22. him-trim

SUBTEST F Final-Consonant Blends and Final Digraphs

1. bat-back
2. kid-kick
3. rat-rash
4. fin-fish
5. bad-bath
6. pill-pith
7. let-lend
8. pop-pond
9. pad-pant
10. hill-hint
11. dull-dusk
12. map-mask
13. fill-fist
14. lap-last
15. cask-camp
16. rat-ramp
17. salt-sank
18. cram-crank

SUBTEST A   INITIAL CONSONANTS

name	b	c	d	f	g	h	j	l	m	n	p	r	s	t	w	y
1. _____																
2. _____																
3. _____																
4. _____																
5. _____																
6. _____																
7. _____																
8. _____																
9. _____																
10. _____																
11. _____																
12. _____																

SUBTEST B FINAL CONSONANTS

name	h	d	g	t	p	m	n	b
1. _____								
2. _____								
3. _____								
4. _____								
5. _____								
6. _____								
7. _____								
8. _____								
9. _____								
10. _____								
11. _____								
12. _____								

SUBTEST C   MIDDLE SHORT VOWELS

name   o   i   e   u   a

	o	i	e	u	a
1.					
2.					
3.					
4.					
5.					
6.					
7					
8.					
9.					
10.					
11.					
12.					

SUBTEST D   MIDDLE LONG VOWELS AND VOWEL DIGRAPHS

name	ai	i͟e	a͟e	ea	oa	ou	o͟e	ow
1. _____								
2. _____								
3. _____								
4. _____								
5. _____								
6. _____								
7. _____								
8. _____								
9. _____								
10. _____								
11. _____								
12. _____								

SUBTEST E   INITIAL-CONSONANT BLENDS AND DIGRAPHS

name	th	wh	sh	ch	fl	sl	sk	sw	st	dr	tr
1. _____											
2. _____											
3. _____											
4. _____											
5. _____											
6. _____											
7. _____											
8. _____											
9. _____											
10. _____											
11. _____											
12. _____											

SUBTEST F   FINAL-CONSONANT BLENDS AND DIGRAPHS

name	ek	sh	th	nd	nt	sk	st	mp	nk
1. _____									
2. _____									
3. _____									
4. _____									
5. _____									
6. _____									
7. _____									
8. _____									
9. _____									
10. _____									
11. _____									
12. _____